C-1158   CAREER EXAMINATION SERIES

This is your
PASSBOOK for...

Maintenance Supervisor (Car Equipment)

Test Preparation Study Guide
Questions & Answers

NLC®

NATIONAL LEARNING CORPORATION®

COPYRIGHT NOTICE

This book is SOLELY intended for, is sold ONLY to, and its use is RESTRICTED to individual, bona fide applicants or candidates who qualify by virtue of having seriously filed applications for appropriate license, certificate, professional and/or promotional advancement, higher school matriculation, scholarship, or other legitimate requirements of education and/or governmental authorities.

This book is NOT intended for use, class instruction, tutoring, training, duplication, copying, reprinting, excerption, or adaptation, etc., by:

1) Other publishers
2) Proprietors and/or Instructors of "Coaching" and/or Preparatory Courses
3) Personnel and/or Training Divisions of commercial, industrial, and governmental organizations
4) Schools, colleges, or universities and/or their departments and staffs, including teachers and other personnel
5) Testing Agencies or Bureaus
6) Study groups which seek by the purchase of a single volume to copy and/or duplicate and/or adapt this material for use by the group as a whole without having purchased individual volumes for each of the members of the group
7) Et al.

Such persons would be in violation of appropriate Federal and State statutes.

PROVISION OF LICENSING AGREEMENTS – Recognized educational, commercial, industrial, and governmental institutions and organizations, and others legitimately engaged in educational pursuits, including training, testing, and measurement activities, may address request for a licensing agreement to the copyright owners, who will determine whether, and under what conditions, including fees and charges, the materials in this book may be used them. In other words, a licensing facility exists for the legitimate use of the material in this book on other than an individual basis. However, it is asseverated and affirmed here that the material in this book CANNOT be used without the receipt of the express permission of such a licensing agreement from the Publishers. Inquiries re licensing should be addressed to the company, attention rights and permissions department.

All rights reserved, including the right of reproduction in whole or in part, in any form or by any means, electronic or mechanical, including photocopying, recording, or by any information storage and retrieval system, without permission in writing from the Publisher.

Copyright © 2024 by
National Learning Corporation

212 Michael Drive, Syosset, NY 11791
(516) 921-8888 • www.passbooks.com
E-mail: info@passbooks.com

PUBLISHED IN THE UNITED STATES OF AMERICA

PASSBOOK® SERIES

THE *PASSBOOK® SERIES* has been created to prepare applicants and candidates for the ultimate academic battlefield – the examination room.

At some time in our lives, each and every one of us may be required to take an examination – for validation, matriculation, admission, qualification, registration, certification, or licensure.

Based on the assumption that every applicant or candidate has met the basic formal educational standards, has taken the required number of courses, and read the necessary texts, the *PASSBOOK® SERIES* furnishes the one special preparation which may assure passing with confidence, instead of failing with insecurity. Examination questions – together with answers – are furnished as the basic vehicle for study so that the mysteries of the examination and its compounding difficulties may be eliminated or diminished by a sure method.

This book is meant to help you pass your examination provided that you qualify and are serious in your objective.

The entire field is reviewed through the huge store of content information which is succinctly presented through a provocative and challenging approach – the question-and-answer method.

A climate of success is established by furnishing the correct answers at the end of each test.

You soon learn to recognize types of questions, forms of questions, and patterns of questioning. You may even begin to anticipate expected outcomes.

You perceive that many questions are repeated or adapted so that you can gain acute insights, which may enable you to score many sure points.

You learn how to confront new questions, or types of questions, and to attack them confidently and work out the correct answers.

You note objectives and emphases, and recognize pitfalls and dangers, so that you may make positive educational adjustments.

Moreover, you are kept fully informed in relation to new concepts, methods, practices, and directions in the field.

You discover that you are actually taking the examination all the time: you are preparing for the examination by "taking" an examination, not by reading extraneous and/or supererogatory textbooks.

In short, this PASSBOOK®, used directedly, should be an important factor in helping you to pass your test.

MAINTENANCE SUPERVISOR (CAR EQUIPMENT)

DUTIES

Maintenance Supervisors (Car Equipment) under general supervision, supervise employees who maintain, inspect, test, examine, lubricate, paint, troubleshoot and make repairs and adjustments on any part of Transit's multiple-unit subway cars and subway service cars in the car shops, terminals, yards and on the road. At Assignment Level 1, Maintenance Supervisors (Car Equipment) supervise employees engaged in the maintenance inspection, testing, examination, troubleshooting and repair of subway car body electrical, electronic, mechanical and pneumatic equipment, truck equipment, body and truck brake rigging, electrical and pneumatic brake equipment, subway car bodies and associated components, air conditioning and heating equipment, and electrical and electronic control and motor equipment. Maintenance Supervisors (Car Equipment) maintain and repair subway car washers and shop equipment; operate and maintain lifting and carrying equipment associated with the placement and removal of subway cars and subway car parts; supervise employees performing the cleaning of subway cars and facilities in shops, yards and terminals; keep written and computerized records; prepare reports; and perform related work.

THE TEST

The test will consist of three distinct components: a competitive multiple-choice examination, a qualifying essay test and a qualifying supervising abilities assessment. All three components of the test will be given in a single session on the same day.

The written multiple choice test will cover the inspection, troubleshooting, maintenance and repair procedures of shop equipment; electrical equipment; electronic equipment; mechanical equipment; pneumatic equipment; truck equipment; truck brake rigging; brake equipment; subway car bodies and components; climate control systems such as air conditioning and heating equipment; subway car wheels and axles; subway car door systems; electrical and electronic control and motor equipment on subway cars; road inspection procedures and equipment; safe work procedures including shop and yard safety procedures and lockout/tagout procedures; transit rules, regulations and policies;
track safety procedures; and reading and understanding schematics and prints.

The qualifying supervisory abilities assessment may include questions that assess the following abilities:

- **Planning and Organizing** - Establishing a course of action for yourself and/or others to accomplish a specific goal; planning proper assignments of personnel and appropriate allocation of resources (including the ability to multitask).
- **Delegation** - Utilizing subordinates effectively; allocating decision making and other responsibilities to the appropriate subordinates.
- **Management Control** - Establishing procedures to monitor and/or regulate processes, tasks, or activities of subordinates and job activities and responsibilities; taking action to monitor the results of delegated assignments or projects.
- **Sensitivity** - Actions that indicate a consideration for the feelings and needs of others.
- **Analysis** - Identifying problems, securing relevant information, relating data from different sources, and identifying possible causes of problems.
- **Judgment** - Developing alternative courses of action and making decisions based on logical assumptions that reflect factual information.
- **Decisiveness** - Readiness to make decisions, renders judgments, take action, or commit oneself.
- **Behavioral Flexibility** - Modifying one's approach to most effectively meet the needs of the situation.

HOW TO TAKE A TEST

I. YOU MUST PASS AN EXAMINATION

A. *WHAT EVERY CANDIDATE SHOULD KNOW*

Examination applicants often ask us for help in preparing for the written test. What can I study in advance? What kinds of questions will be asked? How will the test be given? How will the papers be graded?

As an applicant for a civil service examination, you may be wondering about some of these things. Our purpose here is to suggest effective methods of advance study and to describe civil service examinations.

Your chances for success on this examination can be increased if you know how to prepare. Those "pre-examination jitters" can be reduced if you know what to expect. You can even experience an adventure in good citizenship if you know why civil service exams are given.

B. *WHY ARE CIVIL SERVICE EXAMINATIONS GIVEN?*

Civil service examinations are important to you in two ways. As a citizen, you want public jobs filled by employees who know how to do their work. As a job seeker, you want a fair chance to compete for that job on an equal footing with other candidates. The best-known means of accomplishing this two-fold goal is the competitive examination.

Exams are widely publicized throughout the nation. They may be administered for jobs in federal, state, city, municipal, town or village governments or agencies.

Any citizen may apply, with some limitations, such as the age or residence of applicants. Your experience and education may be reviewed to see whether you meet the requirements for the particular examination. When these requirements exist, they are reasonable and applied consistently to all applicants. Thus, a competitive examination may cause you some uneasiness now, but it is your privilege and safeguard.

C. *HOW ARE CIVIL SERVICE EXAMS DEVELOPED?*

Examinations are carefully written by trained technicians who are specialists in the field known as "psychological measurement," in consultation with recognized authorities in the field of work that the test will cover. These experts recommend the subject matter areas or skills to be tested; only those knowledges or skills important to your success on the job are included. The most reliable books and source materials available are used as references. Together, the experts and technicians judge the difficulty level of the questions.

Test technicians know how to phrase questions so that the problem is clearly stated. Their ethics do not permit "trick" or "catch" questions. Questions may have been tried out on sample groups, or subjected to statistical analysis, to determine their usefulness.

Written tests are often used in combination with performance tests, ratings of training and experience, and oral interviews. All of these measures combine to form the best-known means of finding the right person for the right job.

II. HOW TO PASS THE WRITTEN TEST

A. NATURE OF THE EXAMINATION

To prepare intelligently for civil service examinations, you should know how they differ from school examinations you have taken. In school you were assigned certain definite pages to read or subjects to cover. The examination questions were quite detailed and usually emphasized memory. Civil service exams, on the other hand, try to discover your present ability to perform the duties of a position, plus your potentiality to learn these duties. In other words, a civil service exam attempts to predict how successful you will be. Questions cover such a broad area that they cannot be as minute and detailed as school exam questions.

In the public service similar kinds of work, or positions, are grouped together in one "class." This process is known as *position-classification*. All the positions in a class are paid according to the salary range for that class. One class title covers all of these positions, and they are all tested by the same examination.

B. FOUR BASIC STEPS

1) Study the announcement

How, then, can you know what subjects to study? Our best answer is: "Learn as much as possible about the class of positions for which you've applied." The exam will test the knowledge, skills and abilities needed to do the work.

Your most valuable source of information about the position you want is the official exam announcement. This announcement lists the training and experience qualifications. Check these standards and apply only if you come reasonably close to meeting them.

The brief description of the position in the examination announcement offers some clues to the subjects which will be tested. Think about the job itself. Review the duties in your mind. Can you perform them, or are there some in which you are rusty? Fill in the blank spots in your preparation.

Many jurisdictions preview the written test in the exam announcement by including a section called "Knowledge and Abilities Required," "Scope of the Examination," or some similar heading. Here you will find out specifically what fields will be tested.

2) Review your own background

Once you learn in general what the position is all about, and what you need to know to do the work, ask yourself which subjects you already know fairly well and which need improvement. You may wonder whether to concentrate on improving your strong areas or on building some background in your fields of weakness. When the announcement has specified "some knowledge" or "considerable knowledge," or has used adjectives like "beginning principles of…" or "advanced … methods," you can get a clue as to the number and difficulty of questions to be asked in any given field. More questions, and hence broader coverage, would be included for those subjects which are more important in the work. Now weigh your strengths and weaknesses against the job requirements and prepare accordingly.

3) Determine the level of the position

Another way to tell how intensively you should prepare is to understand the level of the job for which you are applying. Is it the entering level? In other words, is this the position in which beginners in a field of work are hired? Or is it an intermediate or advanced level? Sometimes this is indicated by such words as "Junior" or "Senior" in the class title. Other jurisdictions use Roman numerals to designate the level – Clerk I, Clerk II, for example. The word "Supervisor" sometimes appears in the title. If the level is not indicated by the title, check the description of duties. Will you be working under very close supervision, or will you have responsibility for independent decisions in this work?

4) Choose appropriate study materials

Now that you know the subjects to be examined and the relative amount of each subject to be covered, you can choose suitable study materials. For beginning level jobs, or even advanced ones, if you have a pronounced weakness in some aspect of your training, read a modern, standard textbook in that field. Be sure it is up to date and has general coverage. Such books are normally available at your library, and the librarian will be glad to help you locate one. For entry-level positions, questions of appropriate difficulty are chosen – neither highly advanced questions, nor those too simple. Such questions require careful thought but not advanced training.

If the position for which you are applying is technical or advanced, you will read more advanced, specialized material. If you are already familiar with the basic principles of your field, elementary textbooks would waste your time. Concentrate on advanced textbooks and technical periodicals. Think through the concepts and review difficult problems in your field.

These are all general sources. You can get more ideas on your own initiative, following these leads. For example, training manuals and publications of the government agency which employs workers in your field can be useful, particularly for technical and professional positions. A letter or visit to the government department involved may result in more specific study suggestions, and certainly will provide you with a more definite idea of the exact nature of the position you are seeking.

III. KINDS OF TESTS

Tests are used for purposes other than measuring knowledge and ability to perform specified duties. For some positions, it is equally important to test ability to make adjustments to new situations or to profit from training. In others, basic mental abilities not dependent on information are essential. Questions which test these things may not appear as pertinent to the duties of the position as those which test for knowledge and information. Yet they are often highly important parts of a fair examination. For very general questions, it is almost impossible to help you direct your study efforts. What we can do is to point out some of the more common of these general abilities needed in public service positions and describe some typical questions.

1) General information

Broad, general information has been found useful for predicting job success in some kinds of work. This is tested in a variety of ways, from vocabulary lists to questions about current events. Basic background in some field of work, such as sociology or economics, may be sampled in a group of questions. Often these are principles which have become familiar to most persons through exposure rather than through formal training. It is difficult to advise you how to study for these questions; being alert to the world around you is our best suggestion.

2) Verbal ability

An example of an ability needed in many positions is verbal or language ability. Verbal ability is, in brief, the ability to use and understand words. Vocabulary and grammar tests are typical measures of this ability. Reading comprehension or paragraph interpretation questions are common in many kinds of civil service tests. You are given a paragraph of written material and asked to find its central meaning.

3) Numerical ability

Number skills can be tested by the familiar arithmetic problem, by checking paired lists of numbers to see which are alike and which are different, or by interpreting charts and graphs. In the latter test, a graph may be printed in the test booklet which you are asked to use as the basis for answering questions.

4) Observation

A popular test for law-enforcement positions is the observation test. A picture is shown to you for several minutes, then taken away. Questions about the picture test your ability to observe both details and larger elements.

5) Following directions

In many positions in the public service, the employee must be able to carry out written instructions dependably and accurately. You may be given a chart with several columns, each column listing a variety of information. The questions require you to carry out directions involving the information given in the chart.

6) Skills and aptitudes

Performance tests effectively measure some manual skills and aptitudes. When the skill is one in which you are trained, such as typing or shorthand, you can practice. These tests are often very much like those given in business school or high school courses. For many of the other skills and aptitudes, however, no short-time preparation can be made. Skills and abilities natural to you or that you have developed throughout your lifetime are being tested.

Many of the general questions just described provide all the data needed to answer the questions and ask you to use your reasoning ability to find the answers. Your best preparation for these tests, as well as for tests of facts and ideas, is to be at your physical and mental best. You, no doubt, have your own methods of getting into an exam-taking mood and keeping "in shape." The next section lists some ideas on this subject.

IV. KINDS OF QUESTIONS

Only rarely is the "essay" question, which you answer in narrative form, used in civil service tests. Civil service tests are usually of the short-answer type. Full instructions for answering these questions will be given to you at the examination. But in case this is your first experience with short-answer questions and separate answer sheets, here is what you need to know:

1) Multiple-choice Questions

Most popular of the short-answer questions is the "multiple choice" or "best answer" question. It can be used, for example, to test for factual knowledge, ability to solve problems or judgment in meeting situations found at work.

A multiple-choice question is normally one of three types—
- It can begin with an incomplete statement followed by several possible endings. You are to find the one ending which *best* completes the statement, although some of the others may not be entirely wrong.
- It can also be a complete statement in the form of a question which is answered by choosing one of the statements listed.

- It can be in the form of a problem – again you select the best answer.

Here is an example of a multiple-choice question with a discussion which should give you some clues as to the method for choosing the right answer:

When an employee has a complaint about his assignment, the action which will *best* help him overcome his difficulty is to
- A. discuss his difficulty with his coworkers
- B. take the problem to the head of the organization
- C. take the problem to the person who gave him the assignment
- D. say nothing to anyone about his complaint

In answering this question, you should study each of the choices to find which is best. Consider choice "A" – Certainly an employee may discuss his complaint with fellow employees, but no change or improvement can result, and the complaint remains unresolved. Choice "B" is a poor choice since the head of the organization probably does not know what assignment you have been given, and taking your problem to him is known as "going over the head" of the supervisor. The supervisor, or person who made the assignment, is the person who can clarify it or correct any injustice. Choice "C" is, therefore, correct. To say nothing, as in choice "D," is unwise. Supervisors have and interest in knowing the problems employees are facing, and the employee is seeking a solution to his problem.

2) True/False Questions

The "true/false" or "right/wrong" form of question is sometimes used. Here a complete statement is given. Your job is to decide whether the statement is right or wrong.

SAMPLE: A roaming cell-phone call to a nearby city costs less than a non-roaming call to a distant city.

This statement is wrong, or false, since roaming calls are more expensive.

This is not a complete list of all possible question forms, although most of the others are variations of these common types. You will always get complete directions for answering questions. Be sure you understand *how* to mark your answers – ask questions until you do.

V. RECORDING YOUR ANSWERS

Computer terminals are used more and more today for many different kinds of exams.
For an examination with very few applicants, you may be told to record your answers in the test booklet itself. Separate answer sheets are much more common. If this separate answer sheet is to be scored by machine – and this is often the case – it is highly important that you mark your answers correctly in order to get credit.
An electronic scoring machine is often used in civil service offices because of the speed with which papers can be scored. Machine-scored answer sheets must be marked with a pencil, which will be given to you. This pencil has a high graphite content which responds to the electronic scoring machine. As a matter of fact, stray dots may register as answers, so do not let your pencil rest on the answer sheet while you are pondering the correct answer. Also, if your pencil lead breaks or is otherwise defective, ask for another.

Since the answer sheet will be dropped in a slot in the scoring machine, be careful not to bend the corners or get the paper crumpled.

The answer sheet normally has five vertical columns of numbers, with 30 numbers to a column. These numbers correspond to the question numbers in your test booklet. After each number, going across the page are four or five pairs of dotted lines. These short dotted lines have small letters or numbers above them. The first two pairs may also have a "T" or "F" above the letters. This indicates that the first two pairs only are to be used if the questions are of the true-false type. If the questions are multiple choice, disregard the "T" and "F" and pay attention only to the small letters or numbers.

Answer your questions in the manner of the sample that follows:

32. The largest city in the United States is
    A. Washington, D.C.
    B. New York City
    C. Chicago
    D. Detroit
    E. San Francisco

1) Choose the answer you think is best. (New York City is the largest, so "B" is correct.)
2) Find the row of dotted lines numbered the same as the question you are answering. (Find row number 32)
3) Find the pair of dotted lines corresponding to the answer. (Find the pair of lines under the mark "B.")
4) Make a solid black mark between the dotted lines.

VI. BEFORE THE TEST

Common sense will help you find procedures to follow to get ready for an examination. Too many of us, however, overlook these sensible measures. Indeed, nervousness and fatigue have been found to be the most serious reasons why applicants fail to do their best on civil service tests. Here is a list of reminders:

- Begin your preparation early – Don't wait until the last minute to go scurrying around for books and materials or to find out what the position is all about.
- Prepare continuously – An hour a night for a week is better than an all-night cram session. This has been definitely established. What is more, a night a week for a month will return better dividends than crowding your study into a shorter period of time.
- Locate the place of the exam – You have been sent a notice telling you when and where to report for the examination. If the location is in a different town or otherwise unfamiliar to you, it would be well to inquire the best route and learn something about the building.
- Relax the night before the test – Allow your mind to rest. Do not study at all that night. Plan some mild recreation or diversion; then go to bed early and get a good night's sleep.
- Get up early enough to make a leisurely trip to the place for the test – This way unforeseen events, traffic snarls, unfamiliar buildings, etc. will not upset you.
- Dress comfortably – A written test is not a fashion show. You will be known by number and not by name, so wear something comfortable.

- Leave excess paraphernalia at home – Shopping bags and odd bundles will get in your way. You need bring only the items mentioned in the official notice you received; usually everything you need is provided. Do not bring reference books to the exam. They will only confuse those last minutes and be taken away from you when in the test room.
- Arrive somewhat ahead of time – If because of transportation schedules you must get there very early, bring a newspaper or magazine to take your mind off yourself while waiting.
- Locate the examination room – When you have found the proper room, you will be directed to the seat or part of the room where you will sit. Sometimes you are given a sheet of instructions to read while you are waiting. Do not fill out any forms until you are told to do so; just read them and be prepared.
- Relax and prepare to listen to the instructions
- If you have any physical problem that may keep you from doing your best, be sure to tell the test administrator. If you are sick or in poor health, you really cannot do your best on the exam. You can come back and take the test some other time.

VII. AT THE TEST

The day of the test is here and you have the test booklet in your hand. The temptation to get going is very strong. Caution! There is more to success than knowing the right answers. You must know how to identify your papers and understand variations in the type of short-answer question used in this particular examination. Follow these suggestions for maximum results from your efforts:

1) Cooperate with the monitor

The test administrator has a duty to create a situation in which you can be as much at ease as possible. He will give instructions, tell you when to begin, check to see that you are marking your answer sheet correctly, and so on. He is not there to guard you, although he will see that your competitors do not take unfair advantage. He wants to help you do your best.

2) Listen to all instructions

Don't jump the gun! Wait until you understand all directions. In most civil service tests you get more time than you need to answer the questions. So don't be in a hurry. Read each word of instructions until you clearly understand the meaning. Study the examples, listen to all announcements and follow directions. Ask questions if you do not understand what to do.

3) Identify your papers

Civil service exams are usually identified by number only. You will be assigned a number; you must not put your name on your test papers. Be sure to copy your number correctly. Since more than one exam may be given, copy your exact examination title.

4) Plan your time

Unless you are told that a test is a "speed" or "rate of work" test, speed itself is usually not important. Time enough to answer all the questions will be provided, but this does not mean that you have all day. An overall time limit has been set. Divide the total time (in minutes) by the number of questions to determine the approximate time you have for each question.

5) Do not linger over difficult questions

If you come across a difficult question, mark it with a paper clip (useful to have along) and come back to it when you have been through the booklet. One caution if you do this – be sure to skip a number on your answer sheet as well. Check often to be sure that you have not lost your place and that you are marking in the row numbered the same as the question you are answering.

6) Read the questions

Be sure you know what the question asks! Many capable people are unsuccessful because they failed to *read* the questions correctly.

7) Answer all questions

Unless you have been instructed that a penalty will be deducted for incorrect answers, it is better to guess than to omit a question.

8) Speed tests

It is often better NOT to guess on speed tests. It has been found that on timed tests people are tempted to spend the last few seconds before time is called in marking answers at random – without even reading them – in the hope of picking up a few extra points. To discourage this practice, the instructions may warn you that your score will be "corrected" for guessing. That is, a penalty will be applied. The incorrect answers will be deducted from the correct ones, or some other penalty formula will be used.

9) Review your answers

If you finish before time is called, go back to the questions you guessed or omitted to give them further thought. Review other answers if you have time.

10) Return your test materials

If you are ready to leave before others have finished or time is called, take ALL your materials to the monitor and leave quietly. Never take any test material with you. The monitor can discover whose papers are not complete, and taking a test booklet may be grounds for disqualification.

VIII. EXAMINATION TECHNIQUES

1) Read the general instructions carefully. These are usually printed on the first page of the exam booklet. As a rule, these instructions refer to the timing of the examination; the fact that you should not start work until the signal and must stop work at a signal, etc. If there are any *special* instructions, such as a choice of questions to be answered, make sure that you note this instruction carefully.

2) When you are ready to start work on the examination, that is as soon as the signal has been given, read the instructions to each question booklet, underline any key words or phrases, such as *least, best, outline, describe* and the like. In this way you will tend to answer as requested rather than discover on reviewing your paper that you *listed without describing*, that you selected the *worst* choice rather than the *best* choice, etc.

3) If the examination is of the objective or multiple-choice type – that is, each question will also give a series of possible answers: A, B, C or D, and you are called upon to select the best answer and write the letter next to that answer on your answer paper – it is advisable to start answering each question in turn. There may be anywhere from 50 to 100 such questions in the three or four hours allotted and you can see how much time would be taken if you read through all the questions before beginning to answer any. Furthermore, if you come across a question or group of questions which you know would be difficult to answer, it would undoubtedly affect your handling of all the other questions.

4) If the examination is of the essay type and contains but a few questions, it is a moot point as to whether you should read all the questions before starting to answer any one. Of course, if you are given a choice – say five out of seven and the like – then it is essential to read all the questions so you can eliminate the two that are most difficult. If, however, you are asked to answer all the questions, there may be danger in trying to answer the easiest one first because you may find that you will spend too much time on it. The best technique is to answer the first question, then proceed to the second, etc.

5) Time your answers. Before the exam begins, write down the time it started, then add the time allowed for the examination and write down the time it must be completed, then divide the time available somewhat as follows:
   - If 3-1/2 hours are allowed, that would be 210 minutes. If you have 80 objective-type questions, that would be an average of 2-1/2 minutes per question. Allow yourself no more than 2 minutes per question, or a total of 160 minutes, which will permit about 50 minutes to review.
   - If for the time allotment of 210 minutes there are 7 essay questions to answer, that would average about 30 minutes a question. Give yourself only 25 minutes per question so that you have about 35 minutes to review.

6) The most important instruction is to *read each question* and make sure you know what is wanted. The second most important instruction is to *time yourself properly* so that you answer every question. The third most important instruction is to *answer every question*. Guess if you have to but include something for each question. Remember that you will receive no credit for a blank and will probably receive some credit if you write something in answer to an essay question. If you guess a letter – say "B" for a multiple-choice question – you may have guessed right. If you leave a blank as an answer to a multiple-choice question, the examiners may respect your feelings but it will not add a point to your score. Some exams may penalize you for wrong answers, so in such cases *only*, you may not want to guess unless you have some basis for your answer.

7) Suggestions
   a. Objective-type questions
      1. Examine the question booklet for proper sequence of pages and questions
      2. Read all instructions carefully
      3. Skip any question which seems too difficult; return to it after all other questions have been answered
      4. Apportion your time properly; do not spend too much time on any single question or group of questions

5. Note and underline key words – *all, most, fewest, least, best, worst, same, opposite*, etc.
6. Pay particular attention to negatives
7. Note unusual option, e.g., unduly long, short, complex, different or similar in content to the body of the question
8. Observe the use of "hedging" words – *probably, may, most likely,* etc.
9. Make sure that your answer is put next to the same number as the question
10. Do not second-guess unless you have good reason to believe the second answer is definitely more correct
11. Cross out original answer if you decide another answer is more accurate; do not erase until you are ready to hand your paper in
12. Answer all questions; guess unless instructed otherwise
13. Leave time for review

b. Essay questions
1. Read each question carefully
2. Determine exactly what is wanted. Underline key words or phrases.
3. Decide on outline or paragraph answer
4. Include many different points and elements unless asked to develop any one or two points or elements
5. Show impartiality by giving pros and cons unless directed to select one side only
6. Make and write down any assumptions you find necessary to answer the questions
7. Watch your English, grammar, punctuation and choice of words
8. Time your answers; don't crowd material

8) Answering the essay question

Most essay questions can be answered by framing the specific response around several key words or ideas. Here are a few such key words or ideas:

M's: manpower, materials, methods, money, management
P's: purpose, program, policy, plan, procedure, practice, problems, pitfalls, personnel, public relations

a. Six basic steps in handling problems:
1. Preliminary plan and background development
2. Collect information, data and facts
3. Analyze and interpret information, data and facts
4. Analyze and develop solutions as well as make recommendations
5. Prepare report and sell recommendations
6. Install recommendations and follow up effectiveness

b. Pitfalls to avoid
1. *Taking things for granted* – A statement of the situation does not necessarily imply that each of the elements is necessarily true; for example, a complaint may be invalid and biased so that all that can be taken for granted is that a complaint has been registered

2. *Considering only one side of a situation* – Wherever possible, indicate several alternatives and then point out the reasons you selected the best one
3. *Failing to indicate follow up* – Whenever your answer indicates action on your part, make certain that you will take proper follow-up action to see how successful your recommendations, procedures or actions turn out to be
4. *Taking too long in answering any single question* – Remember to time your answers properly

IX. AFTER THE TEST

Scoring procedures differ in detail among civil service jurisdictions although the general principles are the same. Whether the papers are hand-scored or graded by machine we have described, they are nearly always graded by number. That is, the person who marks the paper knows only the number – never the name – of the applicant. Not until all the papers have been graded will they be matched with names. If other tests, such as training and experience or oral interview ratings have been given, scores will be combined. Different parts of the examination usually have different weights. For example, the written test might count 60 percent of the final grade, and a rating of training and experience 40 percent. In many jurisdictions, veterans will have a certain number of points added to their grades.

After the final grade has been determined, the names are placed in grade order and an eligible list is established. There are various methods for resolving ties between those who get the same final grade – probably the most common is to place first the name of the person whose application was received first. Job offers are made from the eligible list in the order the names appear on it. You will be notified of your grade and your rank as soon as all these computations have been made. This will be done as rapidly as possible.

People who are found to meet the requirements in the announcement are called "eligibles." Their names are put on a list of eligible candidates. An eligible's chances of getting a job depend on how high he stands on this list and how fast agencies are filling jobs from the list.

When a job is to be filled from a list of eligibles, the agency asks for the names of people on the list of eligibles for that job. When the civil service commission receives this request, it sends to the agency the names of the three people highest on this list. Or, if the job to be filled has specialized requirements, the office sends the agency the names of the top three persons who meet these requirements from the general list.

The appointing officer makes a choice from among the three people whose names were sent to him. If the selected person accepts the appointment, the names of the others are put back on the list to be considered for future openings.

That is the rule in hiring from all kinds of eligible lists, whether they are for typist, carpenter, chemist, or something else. For every vacancy, the appointing officer has his choice of any one of the top three eligibles on the list. This explains why the person whose name is on top of the list sometimes does not get an appointment when some of the persons lower on the list do. If the appointing officer chooses the second or third eligible, the No. 1 eligible does not get a job at once, but stays on the list until he is appointed or the list is terminated.

X. HOW TO PASS THE INTERVIEW TEST

The examination for which you applied requires an oral interview test. You have already taken the written test and you are now being called for the interview test – the final part of the formal examination.

You may think that it is not possible to prepare for an interview test and that there are no procedures to follow during an interview. Our purpose is to point out some things you can do in advance that will help you and some good rules to follow and pitfalls to avoid while you are being interviewed.

What is an interview supposed to test?

The written examination is designed to test the technical knowledge and competence of the candidate; the oral is designed to evaluate intangible qualities, not readily measured otherwise, and to establish a list showing the relative fitness of each candidate – as measured against his competitors – for the position sought. Scoring is not on the basis of "right" and "wrong," but on a sliding scale of values ranging from "not passable" to "outstanding." As a matter of fact, it is possible to achieve a relatively low score without a single "incorrect" answer because of evident weakness in the qualities being measured.

Occasionally, an examination may consist entirely of an oral test – either an individual or a group oral. In such cases, information is sought concerning the technical knowledges and abilities of the candidate, since there has been no written examination for this purpose. More commonly, however, an oral test is used to supplement a written examination.

Who conducts interviews?

The composition of oral boards varies among different jurisdictions. In nearly all, a representative of the personnel department serves as chairman. One of the members of the board may be a representative of the department in which the candidate would work. In some cases, "outside experts" are used, and, frequently, a businessman or some other representative of the general public is asked to serve. Labor and management or other special groups may be represented. The aim is to secure the services of experts in the appropriate field.

However the board is composed, it is a good idea (and not at all improper or unethical) to ascertain in advance of the interview who the members are and what groups they represent. When you are introduced to them, you will have some idea of their backgrounds and interests, and at least you will not stutter and stammer over their names.

What should be done before the interview?

While knowledge about the board members is useful and takes some of the surprise element out of the interview, there is other preparation which is more substantive. It *is* possible to prepare for an oral interview – in several ways:

1) Keep a copy of your application and review it carefully before the interview

This may be the only document before the oral board, and the starting point of the interview. Know what education and experience you have listed there, and the sequence and dates of all of it. Sometimes the board will ask you to review the highlights of your experience for them; you should not have to hem and haw doing it.

2) Study the class specification and the examination announcement

Usually, the oral board has one or both of these to guide them. The qualities, characteristics or knowledges required by the position sought are stated in these documents. They offer valuable clues as to the nature of the oral interview. For example, if the job involves supervisory responsibilities, the announcement will usually indicate that knowledge of modern supervisory methods and the qualifications of the candidate as a supervisor will be tested. If so, you can expect such questions, frequently in the form of a hypothetical situation which you are expected to solve. NEVER go into an oral without knowledge of the duties and responsibilities of the job you seek.

3) Think through each qualification required

Try to visualize the kind of questions you would ask if you were a board member. How well could you answer them? Try especially to appraise your own knowledge and background in each area, *measured against the job sought*, and identify any areas in which you are weak. Be critical and realistic – do not flatter yourself.

4) Do some general reading in areas in which you feel you may be weak

For example, if the job involves supervision and your past experience has NOT, some general reading in supervisory methods and practices, particularly in the field of human relations, might be useful. Do NOT study agency procedures or detailed manuals. The oral board will be testing your understanding and capacity, not your memory.

5) Get a good night's sleep and watch your general health and mental attitude

You will want a clear head at the interview. Take care of a cold or any other minor ailment, and of course, no hangovers.

What should be done on the day of the interview?

Now comes the day of the interview itself. Give yourself plenty of time to get there. Plan to arrive somewhat ahead of the scheduled time, particularly if your appointment is in the fore part of the day. If a previous candidate fails to appear, the board might be ready for you a bit early. By early afternoon an oral board is almost invariably behind schedule if there are many candidates, and you may have to wait. Take along a book or magazine to read, or your application to review, but leave any extraneous material in the waiting room when you go in for your interview. In any event, relax and compose yourself.

The matter of dress is important. The board is forming impressions about you – from your experience, your manners, your attitude, and your appearance. Give your personal appearance careful attention. Dress your best, but not your flashiest. Choose conservative, appropriate clothing, and be sure it is immaculate. This is a business interview, and your appearance should indicate that you regard it as such. Besides, being well groomed and properly dressed will help boost your confidence.

Sooner or later, someone will call your name and escort you into the interview room. *This is it.* From here on you are on your own. It is too late for any more preparation. But remember, you asked for this opportunity to prove your fitness, and you are here because your request was granted.

What happens when you go in?

The usual sequence of events will be as follows: The clerk (who is often the board stenographer) will introduce you to the chairman of the oral board, who will introduce you to the other members of the board. Acknowledge the introductions before you sit down. Do not be surprised if you find a microphone facing you or a stenotypist sitting by. Oral interviews are usually recorded in the event of an appeal or other review.

Usually the chairman of the board will open the interview by reviewing the highlights of your education and work experience from your application – primarily for the benefit of the other members of the board, as well as to get the material into the record. Do not interrupt or comment unless there is an error or significant misinterpretation; if that is the case, do not hesitate. But do not quibble about insignificant matters. Also, he will usually ask you some question about your education, experience or your present job – partly to get you to start talking and to establish the interviewing "rapport." He may start the actual questioning, or turn it over to one of the other members. Frequently, each member undertakes the questioning on a particular area, one in which he is perhaps most competent, so you can expect each member to participate in the examination. Because time is limited, you may also expect some rather abrupt switches in the direction the questioning takes, so do not be upset by it. Normally, a board member will not pursue a single line of questioning unless he discovers a particular strength or weakness.

After each member has participated, the chairman will usually ask whether any member has any further questions, then will ask you if you have anything you wish to add. Unless you are expecting this question, it may floor you. Worse, it may start you off on an extended, extemporaneous speech. The board is not usually seeking more information. The question is principally to offer you a last opportunity to present further qualifications or to indicate that you have nothing to add. So, if you feel that a significant qualification or characteristic has been overlooked, it is proper to point it out in a sentence or so. Do not compliment the board on the thoroughness of their examination – they have been sketchy, and you know it. If you wish, merely say, "No thank you, I have nothing further to add." This is a point where you can "talk yourself out" of a good impression or fail to present an important bit of information. Remember, *you close the interview yourself.*

The chairman will then say, "That is all, Mr. _____, thank you." Do not be startled; the interview is over, and quicker than you think. Thank him, gather your belongings and take your leave. Save your sigh of relief for the other side of the door.

How to put your best foot forward

Throughout this entire process, you may feel that the board individually and collectively is trying to pierce your defenses, seek out your hidden weaknesses and embarrass and confuse you. Actually, this is not true. They are obliged to make an appraisal of your qualifications for the job you are seeking, and they want to see you in your best light. Remember, they must interview all candidates and a non-cooperative candidate may become a failure in spite of their best efforts to bring out his qualifications. Here are 15 suggestions that will help you:

1) Be natural – Keep your attitude confident, not cocky

If you are not confident that you can do the job, do not expect the board to be. Do not apologize for your weaknesses, try to bring out your strong points. The board is interested in a positive, not negative, presentation. Cockiness will antagonize any board member and make him wonder if you are covering up a weakness by a false show of strength.

2) Get comfortable, but don't lounge or sprawl

Sit erectly but not stiffly. A careless posture may lead the board to conclude that you are careless in other things, or at least that you are not impressed by the importance of the occasion. Either conclusion is natural, even if incorrect. Do not fuss with your clothing, a pencil or an ashtray. Your hands may occasionally be useful to emphasize a point; do not let them become a point of distraction.

3) Do not wisecrack or make small talk

This is a serious situation, and your attitude should show that you consider it as such. Further, the time of the board is limited – they do not want to waste it, and neither should you.

4) Do not exaggerate your experience or abilities

In the first place, from information in the application or other interviews and sources, the board may know more about you than you think. Secondly, you probably will not get away with it. An experienced board is rather adept at spotting such a situation, so do not take the chance.

5) If you know a board member, do not make a point of it, yet do not hide it

Certainly you are not fooling him, and probably not the other members of the board. Do not try to take advantage of your acquaintanceship – it will probably do you little good.

6) Do not dominate the interview

Let the board do that. They will give you the clues – do not assume that you have to do all the talking. Realize that the board has a number of questions to ask you, and do not try to take up all the interview time by showing off your extensive knowledge of the answer to the first one.

7) Be attentive

You only have 20 minutes or so, and you should keep your attention at its sharpest throughout. When a member is addressing a problem or question to you, give him your undivided attention. Address your reply principally to him, but do not exclude the other board members.

8) Do not interrupt

A board member may be stating a problem for you to analyze. He will ask you a question when the time comes. Let him state the problem, and wait for the question.

9) Make sure you understand the question

Do not try to answer until you are sure what the question is. If it is not clear, restate it in your own words or ask the board member to clarify it for you. However, do not haggle about minor elements.

10) Reply promptly but not hastily

A common entry on oral board rating sheets is "candidate responded readily," or "candidate hesitated in replies." Respond as promptly and quickly as you can, but do not jump to a hasty, ill-considered answer.

11) Do not be peremptory in your answers

A brief answer is proper – but do not fire your answer back. That is a losing game from your point of view. The board member can probably ask questions much faster than you can answer them.

12) Do not try to create the answer you think the board member wants

He is interested in what kind of mind you have and how it works – not in playing games. Furthermore, he can usually spot this practice and will actually grade you down on it.

13) Do not switch sides in your reply merely to agree with a board member

Frequently, a member will take a contrary position merely to draw you out and to see if you are willing and able to defend your point of view. Do not start a debate, yet do not surrender a good position. If a position is worth taking, it is worth defending.

14) Do not be afraid to admit an error in judgment if you are shown to be wrong

The board knows that you are forced to reply without any opportunity for careful consideration. Your answer may be demonstrably wrong. If so, admit it and get on with the interview.

15) Do not dwell at length on your present job

The opening question may relate to your present assignment. Answer the question but do not go into an extended discussion. You are being examined for a *new* job, not your present one. As a matter of fact, try to phrase ALL your answers in terms of the job for which you are being examined.

Basis of Rating

Probably you will forget most of these "do's" and "don'ts" when you walk into the oral interview room. Even remembering them all will not ensure you a passing grade. Perhaps you did not have the qualifications in the first place. But remembering them will help you to put your best foot forward, without treading on the toes of the board members.

Rumor and popular opinion to the contrary notwithstanding, an oral board wants you to make the best appearance possible. They know you are under pressure – but they also want to see how you respond to it as a guide to what your reaction would be under the pressures of the job you seek. They will be influenced by the degree of poise you display, the personal traits you show and the manner in which you respond.

ABOUT THIS BOOK

This book contains tests divided into Examination Sections. Go through each test, answering every question in the margin. We have also attached a sample answer sheet at the back of the book that can be removed and used. At the end of each test look at the answer key and check your answers. On the ones you got wrong, look at the right answer choice and learn. Do not fill in the answers first. Do not memorize the questions and answers, but understand the answer and principles involved. On your test, the questions will likely be different from the samples. Questions are changed and new ones added. If you understand these past questions you should have success with any changes that arise. Tests may consist of several types of questions. We have additional books on each subject should more study be advisable or necessary for you. Finally, the more you study, the better prepared you will be. This book is intended to be the last thing you study before you walk into the examination room. Prior study of relevant texts is also recommended. NLC publishes some of these in our Fundamental Series. Knowledge and good sense are important factors in passing your exam. Good luck also helps. So now study this Passbook, absorb the material contained within and take that knowledge into the examination. Then do your best to pass that exam.

EXAMINATION SECTION

EXAMINATION SECTION
TEST 1

DIRECTIONS: Each question or incomplete statement is followed by several suggested answers or completions. Select the one that BEST answers the question or completes the statement. *PRINT THE LETTER OF THE CORRECT ANSWER IN THE SPACE AT THE RIGHT.*

1. In coupling the traction motor to the track axle reduction gear, compensation is made for the PROPER
    A. center to center distance between pinion and gear
    B. backlash between pinion and gear
    C. alignment of the motor with the pinion
    D. motor bearing clearance

   1.____

2. The MAIN purpose of the motor-generator set on a subway car is to
    A. provide energy for operating the air compressors
    B. provide energy for heating the cars
    C. convert third rail voltage to battery voltage
    D. provide energy for the air conditioning system

   2.____

3. The motorman's bypass in the R-38 subway car is used to bypass the
    A. signal light relay   B. door relay
    C. pilot valve   D. master controller

   3.____

4. The D6 wire in the subway train wiring is part of the _____ circuit.
    A. DI wire   B. guard light
    C. motorman's indication   D. conductor's indication

   4.____

5. A metal sheet is to have a row of ten holes drilled parallel to its length. The holes are to be 3½" in diameter and spaced 5½" on centers. The distance from the edge of each end hole to the adjacent edge of the sheet is to be the same distance as the distance between the edges of the other holes. Based on this information, the sheet should have a MINIMUM length of
    A. 4'8¾"   B. 4'9"   C. 5'6½"   D. 5'9¾"

   5.____

6. With respect to the various operating positions of the master controller in the R-10 through R-22 subway cars, FULL third rail voltage is applied to each individual traction motor in _____ position(s).
    A. the switching   B. the series
    C. the parallel   D. none of the master controller

   6.____

7. Spot welding is MOST commonly used to
    A. hold I-beams together
    B. fasten thin gauge metal sheets together
    C. weld thick aluminum plates together
    D. make joints watertight

   7.____

8. It is required that a 1 ¾" diameter shaft be machined to within a tolerance of plus or minus two-thousandths of an inch. The machined shaft will have to be rejected if it has a diameter of
   A. 1.746"   B. 1.748"   C. 1.750"   D. 1.752"

9. Some subway cars have a timer in the control circuit to regulate the
   A. air compressors
   B. guard light
   C. fluorescent lights
   D. cab heaters

10. The number of electrical pins in each of the two electric coupler boxes on an R-44 car is
    A. 39   B. 48   C. 52   D. 59

11. On the R-12 type trains set up for one-man conductor operation, the number of drum switches that MUST be in the *thru* position on a ten-car train is
    A. 15   B. 16   C. 18   D. 20

12. To ensure proper lubrication of the subway car air conditioning refrigerant compressor, the proper level of the lubricating oil in the crankcase must be maintained. The FIRST step that should be taken in the process of adding oil to the crankcase is to
    A. empty the compressor of the refrigerant
    B. pump all the refrigerant into the compressor with the compressor discharge valve closed
    C. remove the filter-drier assembly
    D. close both of the expansion valves

13. The expansion of the refrigerant into the subway car air conditioning evaporator is accomplished with
    A. one expansion valve
    B. two expansion valves
    C. one capillary tube
    D. one capillary tube and one expansion valve

14. If a heavy arc is drawn when the main knife switch on a subway car is opened, then the MOST likely cause of the arc is
    A. a defective contact on the knife switch
    B. the electrical load which was not removed from the circuit
    C. a defective circuit breaker in the circuit
    D. the fuse in the circuit is overrated

15. After a car has been serviced by the wheel truing machine, it is MOST important to
    A. gauge the contact shoes
    B. check the axle bearings
    C. realign the traction motor coupling
    D. check the setting of the variable load valve

16. A subway car of the R-10 to R-22 type has an open circuited armature in one of its four motors. When putting this car on test in the car shop, the car should take motor power in _____ position(s).
    A. the switching
    B. the series
    C. the parallel
    D. none of the master controller

16._____

17. The area of the steel plate shown in the sketch at the right is _____ sq.ft.
    A. 16
    B. 18
    C. 20
    D. 22.

17._____

18. The subway lines which require that the correct free height of the contact shoe pad above the top of the running rail be 2¾" are the
    A. IND and IRT
    B. IND and BMT
    C. IRT and BMT
    D. IND, IRT and BMT

18._____

19. Overtime hours worked by personnel in the Cars and Shops Department are recorded on colored cards. The color of the overtime card which should be submitted for a maintainer is
    A. blue
    B. yellow
    C. white
    D. pink

19._____

20. It is important to maintain the subway air conditioning refrigeration system free of moisture. Slight amounts of water in the refrigerant will lead to
    A. hydraulic lock in the compressor cylinder
    B. early deterioration of the refrigerant
    C. freezing and plugging of the expansion valves
    D. deterioration of the sweated joints of the copper fittings

20._____

21. One of the functions of the electric heat assembly which is mounted in the downstream airflow of the subway car air conditioning evaporator coil assembly is to
    A. dissipate excess electrical power during low demand loads
    B. provide a sensible load during summer operation for minimizing compressor cycling
    C. protect the electric motor against application of voltages above rated value
    D. heat the car during winter operation to standard temperature

21._____

22. A *rolling test* is made on a train to make certain that
    A. the traction motors are in good condition
    B. working voltage is available
    C. the brakes are free
    D. the axle bearings are lubricated

    22._____

23. The car device which permits electrical control of pneumatic brake equipment is the _____ valve.
    A. application and release
    B. feed
    C. charging
    D. thermistor

    23._____

24. Car inspections are identified with the letters A, B, and C. These letters indicate the
    A. type of cars being inspected
    B. division in which the cars operate
    C. mileage at which the particular inspection is to be made
    D. shop in which the inspection is to be made

    24._____

25. One of the component parts of the A-I compressor unit is the _____ valve.
    A. lockout magnet
    B. main reservoir safety
    C. relay
    D. thermal control

    25._____

KEY (CORRECT ANSWERS)

1.	C		11.	B
2.	C		12.	A
3.	B		13.	B
4.	D		14.	B
5.	B		15.	A
6.	D		16.	C
7.	B		17.	C
8.	A		18.	B
9.	C		19.	B
10.	D		20.	C

21. B
22. C
23. A
24. C
25. B

TEST 2

DIRECTIONS: Each question or incomplete statement is followed by several suggested answers or completions. Select the one that BEST answers the question or completes the statement. *PRINT THE LETTER OF THE CORRECT ANSWER IN THE SPACE AT THE RIGHT.*

1. The designation for the couplers on R-10 to R-22 cars is   1.____
   A. H2C   B. H2A   C. JI   D. OB

2. A subway car contact shoe which is adjusted too low would MOST likely cause trouble   2.____
   A. when the train is moving over a section break in the third rail
   B. when the train is starting up after a station stop
   C. by striking the trip on the road bed
   D. by striking the signal box on the road bed

3. One of the functions of the *variable load valve* on the R-22 subway car is to limit the air pressure that is delivered to the   3.____
   A. J relay valve   B. SR relay
   C. B relay valve   D. BP relay

4. A car part made by a manufacturer X has a purchase cost of $7,500 and a life of five years. It requires a yearly maintenance cost of $50. Manufacturer J offers a similar part of this type for $4,800, with a life of three years and a yearly maintenance cost of $75. By purchasing the part offering a better overall value, the yearly SAVINGS per unit purchased would be   4.____
   A. $115   B. $125   C. $135   D. $140

5. In operation, subway car wheels can get loose and move along their axle. To check for this wheel movement, a back to back wheel gage is used. The wheel location on the axle can be considered to be satisfactory if the measurement with this gage is between _____ maximum and _____ minimum.   5.____
   A. 52½"; 52¼"   B. 53⅜"; 53¼"
   C. 54½"; 54⅜"   D. 54¾"; 53⅝"

6. On the R-38 type cars, in order to test the operation of the reset magnet, during a B inspection, the inspector SHOULD   6.____
   A. move the brake handle to the EMERGENCY position
   B. put a block under the load sensor lever arm
   C. remove the No. 2 wire jumper ground connection
   D. place a door operator cut-out switch to the OFF position

7. On the R-38 type cars, while the brake pipe pressure is at 110 psi, if the inspector puts the master controller down and then moves the brake valve handle to the *release* position, the duplex gage for the straight air pressure SHOULD read _____ psi.   7.____
   A. 0   B. 75   C. 80   D. 110

Questions 8-13.

DIRECTIONS: Questions 8 through 13 are to be answered on the basis of the two views of the bracket shown below. Consult this drawing when answering these questions.

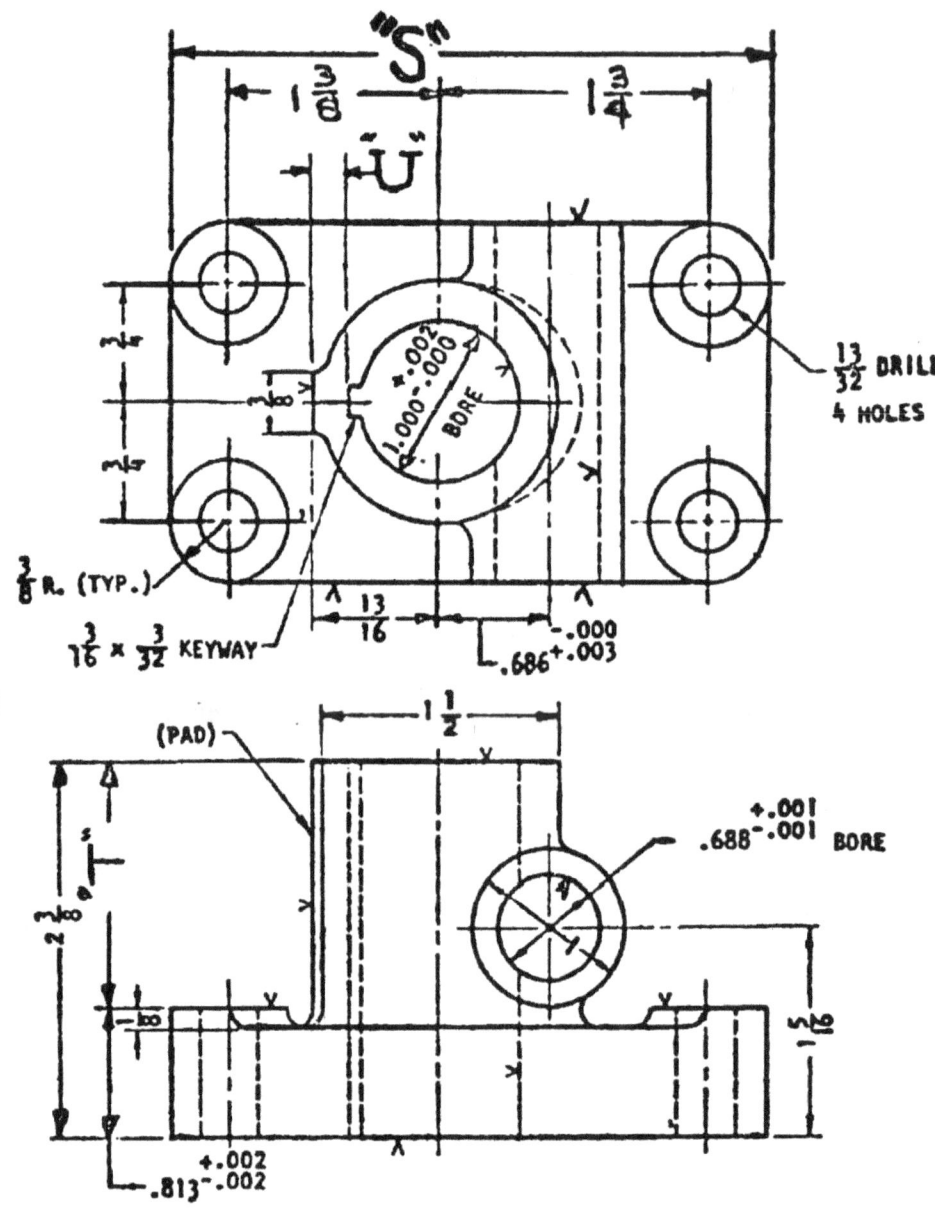

ALL DIMENSIONS IN INCHES

BRACKET

3 (#2)

8. The nominal dimension T is
   A. 1 17/32"   B. 1 9/16"   C. 1 19/32"   D. 1 11/15"

9. The nominal dimension S is
   A. 3 3/8"   B. 3 5/8"   C. 3 7/8"   D. 4 1/8"

10. A bushing is to be press fitted into the .688" bored hole with an .001" to .004" interference fit. The outside diameter of the bushing should be
    A. .687" to .689"
    B. .688" to .690"
    C. .690" to .691"
    D. .691" to .693"

11. A shaft with an outside diameter is to be assembled into the bored hole The clearance between the shaft and hole is
    A. .001" to .003"
    B. .002" to .004"
    C. .002" to .005"
    D. .002" to .006"

12. The dimension U is MOST NEARLY
    A. 5/32"   B. 7/32"   C. 7/16"   D. 5/8"

13. The cross-sectional dimensions of the key stock that would be required for the keyway in the vertical bore are
    A. 3/32" x 3/32"
    B. 3/32" to 3/16"
    C. 3/16" x 3/16"
    D. 3/8" x 3/8"

14. On the R-44 subway cars, the equipment associated with the A and/or B car is
    A. motor-generator and batteries on the A car, air compressor on the B car
    B. air compressor on the A car, motor-generator and batteries on the B car
    C. air compressor and batteries on the A car, pneumatic operating units on both cars
    D. air compressor and batteries on the B car, pneumatic operating units on both cars

15. The toggle switch used to cut out an electric door operator on R-12 to R-38 cars is located
    A. under a seat
    B. in a wall panel
    C. in the No. 1 cab
    D. in the No. 2 cab

16. The recommended signaling method for an inspector to use for stopping a moving train with a hand-held light is to
    A. move the light to and fro across the track
    B. move the light up and down over the track
    C. hold the light in one hand away from the body and stand on the side of the track
    D. place th3e light on the road bed in the center of the track

17. An emergency alarm box should be pulled by an inspector in order to
    A. start up the subway emergency ventilating fans
    B. remove third rail power
    C. open all car doors
    D. notify the passengers of danger

18. Of the following, the car trouble which causes the MOST frequent train delays is defective
    A. traction motors   B. motor controllers
    C. doors   D. brakes

19. A car with a grounded train line wire is BEST isolated from the other cars by
    A. opening the control cut-out switch
    B. opening the main knife switch
    C. retrieving the electric portions
    D. slippering all the contact shoes

20. A car part can be overhauled at the rate of 12 parts per hour. Each part requires new material costing $3 each. If the labor cost if $7 per hour, one part an be overhauled for a TOTAL cost (labor plus material) of MOST NEARLY
    A. $3.32   B. $3.58   C. $3.73   D. $4.10

21. After the wheels of a subway car wear sufficiently, it may be necessary to compensate for wheel wear by readjusting the
    A. bolster height   B. equalizer spring height
    C. equalizer bar   D. journal box

22. On R-44 cars equipped with the RT-5C brake system, the black needle of the duplex air gage indicates _____ pressure.
    A. brake pipe   B. straight air pipe
    C. brake cylinder   D. main reservoir air

23. Of the following, the defective wheel which is LEAST likely to be corrected on the wheel truing machine is a _____ wheel.
    A. thin flange   B. built-up tread
    C. limit   D. vertical flange

24. The R-44 cars have a device called a decelostat. The purpose of this device is to
    A. permit the train to make a smooth stop
    B. prevent the train from overspeeding
    C. allow the train to decelerate before entering the dynamic braking phase
    D. minimize sliding of the wheels

25. A maintainer in the Car Maintenance Department who returns to work after an absence due to sickness must file a sick-leave application within _____ hours after his return to work.
   A. 24 B. 48 C. 72 D. 96

KEY (CORRECT ANSWERS)

1. A
2. A
3. C
4. B
5. B

6. D
7. A
8. B
9. C
10. C

11. C
12. B
13. C
14. C
15. A

16. A
17. B
18. C
19. C
20. B

21. A
22. A
23. C
24. D
25. C

TEST 3

DIRECTIONS: Each question or incomplete statement is followed by several suggested answers or completions. Select the one that BEST answers the question or completes the statement. *PRINT THE LETTER OF THE CORRECT ANSWER IN THE SPACE AT THE RIGHT.*

Questions 1-2.

DIRECTIONS: Questions 1 and 2 apply to the Transit Authority Graffiti Removal Program.

1. The amount of solvent required per car per application for removing graffiti is MOST NEARLY _____ to _____ gallons.
   A. 2; 3
   B. 5; 6
   C. 8; 9
   D. 10; 12

   1._____

2. A car which had a complete paint job four weeks ago is found marked on the exterior surface with heavy graffiti. The recommended time period for removing the graffiti with solvent and machine washing is
   A. within 3 days
   B. within 1 week
   C. within 2 weeks
   D. only after 2 or more weeks

   2._____

3. Closing the double cut-out cock on a subway car of the R-1 to R-9 type cuts out the brakes
   A. of that car only
   B. on the two adjacent cars only
   C. on the end cars only
   D. on all cars

   3._____

4. A car part costs $150 per 50 units when purchased in a finished condition from a vendor. The car part can be made in the shop at a total cost of $2.20 per unit, when made on a machine which can be purchased for $1,000. The MINIMUM number of parts which must be made on this machine before the savings equal the cost of the machine is
   A. 850
   B. 1,000
   C. 1,250
   D. 1,500

   4._____

5. The eyeglasses which certain maintainers wear throughout the day are called *safety glasses* because of their construction which makes them
   A. less likely than regular eyeglasses to shatter when struck by a hard object
   B. unsuitable for reading written instructional material
   C. more effective than goggles for keeping particles from the eyes
   D. suitable for eliminating the glare of overhead lights

   5._____

6. A shim pack is to be assembled having an overall thickness between the limits of 0.250" and 0.253". If individual shims are available in thicknesses of 0.005", 0.014", and 0.016", the MINIMUM number of shims required to make up the assembly in any combination is
   A. 18
   B. 17
   C. 16
   D. 15

   6._____

7. A car wheel wears such that the diameter is reduced from 34 inches to 33¾ inches after 150,000 miles of operation. The rate of wear of the car wheel on the diameter is _____ of an inch per _____ miles.
   A. ¹/₁₅₀; 1,000
   B. ¹/₆; 100,000
   C. ⁵/₆; 250,000
   D. ⁴/₅; 500,000

   7.____

8. After R-40 cars are coupled, the electric portion slide will automatically unlock when the brake valve handle is placed in _____ position.
   A. running release
   B. full release
   C. handle off
   D. full service

   8.____

9. The application and release magnet valves on the type R-44 car are actuated by
   A. the camshaft assembly in the brake valve
   B. an electrical signal from the electronic operating unit
   C. the pneumatic self-lapping portion of the brake valve
   D. the pneumatic operating unit

   9.____

10. Track gauge means the distance between the
    A. signal rail and third rail
    B. two running rails
    C. heights of the track in each 100 feet of track
    D. third rail and the adjacent running rail

    10.____

11. Whenever a feed valve is repaired or replaced on a subway car, it must be properly identified on the repair card by listing the _____ number.
    A. store's department code
    B. manufacturer's part
    C. component code
    D. air brake

    11.____

12. Before a car wheel is mounted on an axle, it is necessary that there be the necessary press fit between wheel and axle. Before mounting the car wheel, it is MOST desirable to machine _____ of the excess material from the _____ and _____ from the _____.
    A. all; wheel bore; none; axle
    B. ¹/₃; axle; ²/₃; wheel bore
    C. ²/₃; axle; ¹/₃; wheel bore
    D. all; axle; none; wheel bore

    12.____

13. Recent statistics on accidents in the Car Maintenance Department reveal that the LARGEST number of accidents are listed in the accident category of
    A. lifting
    B. trips and falls
    C. smoke inhalation
    D. chemical burns

    13.____

14. A COMMON cause of flat spots on the wheels of R-42 subway cars is a(n)
    A. defective lock-out magnet
    B. actuation of the trip cock
    C. defective reset magnet valve
    D. actuation of the conductor's valve

    14.____

15. If a foreman is planning a 12-month vacation schedule for his men, a GOOD way for him to estimate the number of man-hours required to cover the scheduled work for this period is for the foreman to
    A. ask each maintainer to estimate the man-hours required on his job
    B. ask his supervisor to estimate the number of man-hours required for each job
    C. run a time study check on each operation in his area
    D. check the record for a similar period and use the same man-hours for estimating the scheduled work

15.____

16. An Edison-cell storage battery having a 75 ampere-hour capacity is $1/3$ discharged. If a charging rate of 2 ½ amperes is used to recharge the battery, it should be fully charged in APPROXIMATELY _____ hours.
    A. 10   B. 20   C. 30   D. 40

16.____

17. A rheostat is used GENERALLY to
    A. vary the resistance of an electrical circuit
    B. control the direction of fluid flow in a three-way thermostatic valve
    C. regulate the suction pressure to an air compressor
    D. prevent overloading of an air compressor

17.____

18. The reading of the vernier height gage scale shown in the adjacent sketch is MOST NEARLY
    A. 2.055
    B. 2.050
    C. 1.465
    D. 1,455

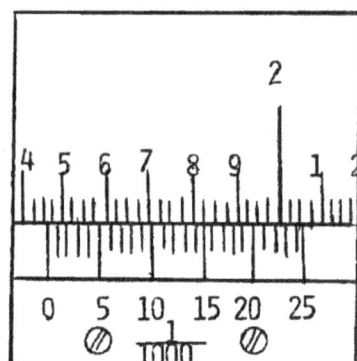

18.____

19. The journal bearings used on a R-44 truck are _____ bearings.
    A. ball   B. brass Babbitt
    C. roller   D. needle

19.____

20. The weight of the 1-inch thick steel plate shown in the sketch to the right is MOST NEARLY _____ pounds.
    A. 2,255
    B. 3,900
    C. 26,700
    D. 53,400

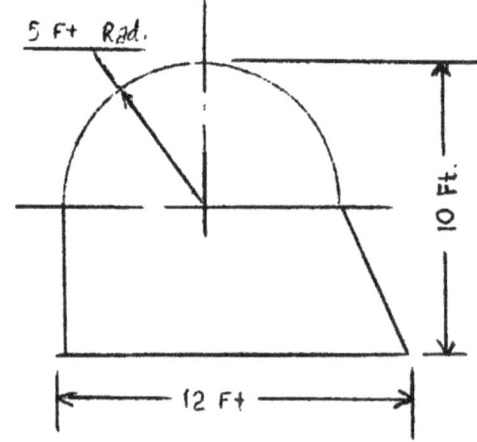

20.____

21. A car inspector should use a contour gage to check the
    A. electric portion of the coupler B. journals
    C. wheels D. axle profile

22. Assume that a foreman has been given a complicated machinery repair job to supervise. He has also been told that this type of job will be done on a continuing basis. He, thereupon, breaks down the repair job into a group of simpler and smaller sub-repair jobs. After he has assigned a particular sub-repair job to a maintainer, he teaches the maintainer different ways of doing the sub-repair job. This procedure is
    A. *good*, because it enables him to pick the one most suited to his abilities
    B. *good*, because it develops greater interest in the work
    C. *poor*, because the single best method should be developed for each sub-repair job
    D. *poor*, because experienced maintainers should decide on how to perform each sub-repair job

23. The action which occurs during dynamic braking of a subway car is that
    A. the traction motors act as generators
    B. the polarity of the motor connections are reversed
    C. a magnetic force is applied to the rails
    D. the traction motors charge the batteries

24. A rivet set is used to
    A. form rivet heads
    B. drill and ream the hole for the rivet
    C. cut the shank length of the rivet
    D. check the rivet strength

25. In the R-44 train, the *P* wire current is controlled by the position of the main handle on the master controller. An interruption of this current will cause
    A. the main circuit breaker to open
    B. a full service brake to be applied on all cars of the train
    C. the emergency lights to go on
    D. the air brake circuit breaker to open

KEY (CORRECT ANSWERS)

1.	B	11.	C
2.	D	12.	A
3.	A	13.	B
4.	C	14.	A
5.	A	15.	D
6.	C	16.	A
7.	C	17.	A
8.	D	18.	C
9.	B	19.	C
10.	B	20.	B

21. C
22. C
23. A
24. A
25. B

———

TEST 4

DIRECTIONS: Each question or incomplete statement is followed by several suggested answers or completions. Select the one that BEST answers the question or completes the statement. *PRINT THE LETTER OF THE CORRECT ANSWER IN THE SPACE AT THE RIGHT.*

1. A pound of a certain type of metal washer contains 360 washers. If ¼ of the material of each washer is removed by enlarging the center of each washer, the number of washers to the pound should then be MOST NEARLY
   A. 280　　　　B. 300　　　　C. 380　　　　D. 480

   1.____

2. A maintainer earns $16.26 per hour, and time and one-half for overtime. Ten percent of his total salary earned is deducted from his paycheck for Social Security and taxes. He also contributes $7.50 per week to a charitable organization. No other deductions are made. If he works 2 hours over his basic 40 hours, his weekly take-home pay should be MOST NEARLY
   A. $699.18　　　B. $629.25　　　C. $621.75　　　D. $615.90

   2.____

3. The PREFERRED agent or device for finding small leaks at the joints of the subway car air conditioning refrigerant lines is
   A. soap suds　　　　　　　B. a halide torch
   C. peppermint oil　　　　　D. titanium oxide smoke

   3.____

4. Refrigerant 22 is used in the subway car air conditioning system. Assume that additional refrigerant is required. The refrigerant can be added in the
   A. liquid state at the discharge side of the condenser
   B. vapor state at the discharge side of the condenser
   C. liquid state at the suction side of the compressor
   D. vapor state before the expansion valve

   4.____

5. An automatic slack adjuster is GENERALLY provided with each
   A. shim box　　　　　B. pneumatic self-lapping valve
   C. brake cylinder　　　D. brake valve

   5.____

6. A guard light that remains son after all the doors of an R-40 train have been closed indicates that
   A. only the motorman's indication is functioning
   B. only the conductor's indication is functioning
   C. both the motorman's and the conductor's indications are functioning
   D. neither the motorman's nor the conductor's indications are functioning

   6.____

7. When moving heavy equipment by means of rollers, it is MOST important to make sure that the
   A. rollers have a diameter less than 4 inches
   B. rollers are well-greased
   C. trailing roller does not suddenly slip out from under the equipment
   D. rollers used are made of steel

   7.____

8. The car equipment which becomes inoperative when third rail power fails is the
   A. motorman's indication light
   B. synchronizing control circuit
   C. door operator motor
   D. potential relay

9. Assume that the average life of a pair of car wheels is 100,000 car-miles, and that 15,000 car miles are lost each time the wheels are turned in the lathe to make them suitable for use. If a certain pair of wheels has been sent to the shop for turning, after 40,000 car-miles and again after 65,000 car-miles of operation, then the number of car-miles of operation REMAINING in the pair of wheels after the second wheel turning is
   A. 0
   B. 5,000
   C. 20,000
   D. 35,000

10. On the ME-43 brake valve, clearance between the application contacts and the pendulum contacts is maintained by adjusting screws which are located in the _____ valve.
    A. deadman's check
    B. electric self-lapping
    C. emergency
    D. pneumatic self-lapping

11. One of the steps in checking the emergency magnet valve (EMV) is to connect a wire jumper on the electric car coupler between the EMV pin and the _____ pin.
    A. BI+
    B. No. 1"
    C. LI
    D. H

12. On R-10 to R-42 subway cars, when a B-3-C conductor's valve is operated, the emergency contactor _____ circuit.
    A. closes the motor generator
    B. closes the dynamic brake
    C. opens the emergency magnet valve
    D. opens the dynamic brake

Questions 13-18.

DIRECTIONS: Questions 13 through 18 are to be answered based on the sketch of the following relay circuit. Consult this drawing when answering these questions.

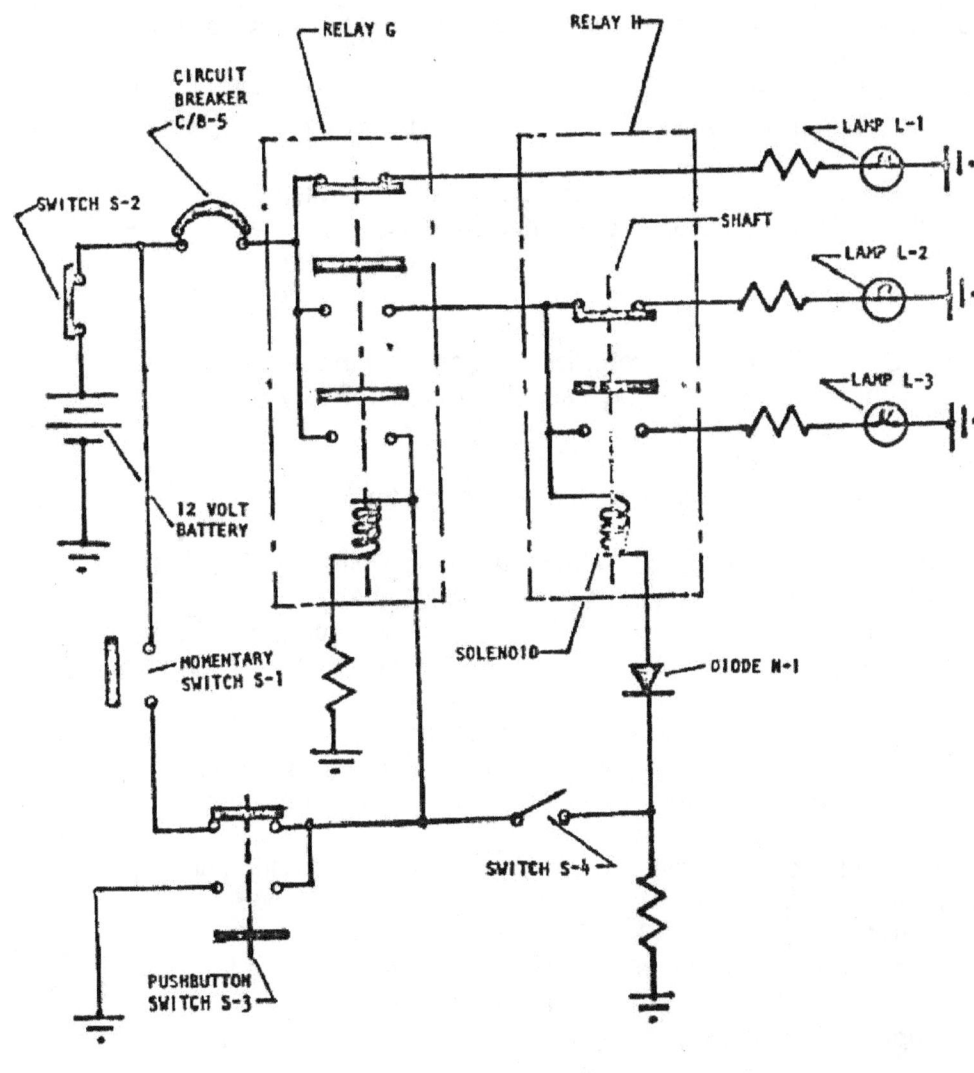

RELAY CIRCUIT

13. With all switches positioned as shown in the above sketch, the condition of the lamps should be such that _____ is lit.
    A. only Lamp L-1
    B. only Lamp L-2
    C. only Lamp L-3
    D. none of the lamps

14. After the momentary switch S-1 is actuated and released, the RESULTING condition of the lamps is such that _____ is(are) lit.
    A. all of the lamps
    B. only Lamp L-1
    C. only Lamp L-2
    D. only Lamp L-3

15. Assume that Relay G has been actuated and the Switch S-4 is closed. The RESULTING condition of the lamps should be such that _____ is(are) lit.
    A. all of the lamps
    B. only Lamp L-1
    C. only Lamp L-2
    D. only Lamp L-3

16. If only Switch S-3 is actuated, then the condition of the lamps should be such that _____ is(are) lit.
    A. only Lamp L-1
    B. only Lamp L-2
    C. both Lamps L-1 and L-2
    D. both Lamps L-1 and L-3

17. Assume that after Relay G has been actuated, the Switch S-3 is actuated. The RESULTING condition of the lamps should be such that _____ is lit.
    A. only Lamp L-1
    B. only Lamp L-2
    C. only Lamp L-3
    D. none of the lamps

18. An IMPORTANT function of the Diode N-I as used in the circuit is to
    A. maintain a constant voltage across the coil of Relay H
    B. prevent Relay H from chattering
    C. limit the current in the coil of Relay H
    D. prevent reverse current from operating Relay H

19. If a car inspector believes that a bad traffic tie-up will result from a car breakdown to which he is sent, he should IMMEDIATELY notify the
    A. station supervisor
    B. superintendent of signals
    C. superintendent of track
    D. control board supervisor

20. A balancing choke is a device used in a subway car
    A. air compressor
    B. brake cylinder hose
    C. door operator control
    D. fan and heat control

21. On trains equipped with dynamic braking, opening of the trip cock on the train will
    A. nullify the dynamic brake
    B. apply both the full dynamic brake and the full air brake
    C. apply a partial air brake and full dynamic brake
    D. apply a full dynamic brake

22. An IMPORTANT advantage of the two-piece contact shoe over a one-piece shoe is that it makes the
    A. inspection of the shoe easier
    B. adjustment of the free height of the shoe easier
    C. replacement of the contact shoe pad easier
    D. shoe contact surface wear longer

23. A car part costs $130 per 100 units if purchased from a vendor. The car part can be made on a machine which can be purchased for $1,000. Assume that this machine has a production life of 20,000 units with no salvage value, and that all shop costs amount to $80 per 100 units turned out in the shop. The money that would be saved during the life of the machine would be
    A. $800 B. $8,000 C. $9,000 D. $18,000

24. A fuse which should not be replaced while a subway car in the inspection barn is connected to third rail voltage is the _____ fuse.
    A. cab light
    B. door
    C. guard light
    D. auxiliary

25. Operation of a subway car with a truck-axle assembly having wheels which differ by $1/8$" or more in diameter would MOST probably result in
    A. loose wheels
    B. thin flanges
    C. cracked flanges
    D. cracked hubs

KEY (CORRECT ANSWERS)

1.	D	11.	A
2.	C	12.	D
3.	B	13.	A
4.	A	14.	D
5.	C	15.	C
6.	D	16.	A
7.	C	17.	D
8.	D	18.	D
9.	B	19.	D
10.	B	20.	B

21. A
22. C
23. C
24. D
25. B

EXAMINATION SECTION
TEST 1

DIRECTIONS: Each question or incomplete statement is followed by several suggested answers or completions. Select the one that BEST answers the question or completes the statement. *PRINT THE LETTER OF THE CORRECT ANSWER IN THE SPACE AT THE RIGHT.*

1. Assume that you are assigned responsibility for the car body painting in one of the main car shops and you are advised that the exterior painting on recently painted cars from this shop is unsatisfactory. Upon inspecting the cars in question, you find that the paint finish shows an excessive amount of sagging and running.
The following painting practices are offered for your consideration as having been possible causes of the runs and sags in the painted finish:
    I. Too much thinner was used.
    II. Too little drying time was allowed between coats.
    III. The spray gun was held too close to the surface of the work.
    IV. The spray gun was held too far away from the surface of the work.
    V. The air pressure used in the spray gun was too low.
    VI. The air pressure used in the spray gun was too high.
    VII. The spray gun was moved too rapidly over the work surface.

    Which of the following suggested answers CORRECTLY lists the possible causes of the runs and sags in the painted finish?

    A. I and IV
    B. IV *only*
    C. I, II, III, V
    D. VI and VII

1.____

2. A foreman has been training a group of newly appointed maintainers in the proper techniques for spray-painting car bodies. Assume that you have been observing these maintainers as they work in order to evaluate how well they have learned to use the spray equipment.
The following practices are offered for your consideration as possibly being indicative of proper spray painting:
A maintainer
    I. swings the spray gun in an arc formed by rotating his body from the hips while holding the spray gun
    II. makes his strokes by moving the spray gun parallel to the surface of the work
    III. holds his gun at right angles to the surface of the work
    IV. keeps a constant 20-inch distance between the gun nozzle and the surface of the work
    V. starts each new stroke underneath the previous stroke so that the edge of each stroke touches only the edge of the preceding stroke

    Which of the following suggested answers CORRECTLY lists the practices indicative of proper spray painting?

    A. I *only*
    B. II and III
    C. III and IV
    D. I, II, III, IV

2.____

21

3. Assume that you are assigned to supervise a welding shop. The following practices are offered for your consideration as possibly appropriate to shop safety in the handling of gas cylinders.
   I. Keep all unused spare pressurized gas cylinders resting on their side in a suitable rack
   II. Provide a manifold for the purpose of centralizing a continuous acetylene supply
   III. Coat the threads on the regulator valve with a light grease when installing it on the cylinder
   IV. Keep the valve protecting caps on the gas cylinder while not in use

   Which of the following suggested answers CORRECTLY lists *unsafe* statements regarding the usage of gas cylinders?

   A. I and III
   B. II and IV
   C. III and IV
   D. I, II, III, IV

4. In the car maintenance department, a five-step management process is suggested for the solution of problems.
   The steps consist of: planning, organizing, controlling, executing, and

   A. achieving
   B. adapting
   C. adjusting
   D. appraising

5. The traction motors for subway cars are of the series type; that is, the motor armature and field are connected in series.
   The following statements of the characteristics of various types of motors are to be reviewed to select those characteristics that are appropriate to series type motors used in subway trains.
   I. Develops a high starting torque
   II. Direction of rotation can be reversed by interchanging the connections of the motor field
   III. Direction of rotation can be reversed by placing the armature and field in parallel
   IV. Speed can be increased by shunting the motor field winding with resistance
   V. Speed can be increased by applying full rail voltage to each motor on the truck

   Which of the following suggested answers lists CORRECT statements of the characteristics of the series type motor which make it appropriate for propelling subway trains?

   A. I *only*
   B. I and II
   C. I, II, IV
   D. I, II, III, IV, V

6. The Woodward height adjuster on a car truck is used to compensate PRIMARILY for

   A. load sensor valve malfunction
   B. wheel wear
   C. journal bearing wear
   D. traction motor pinion and gear misalignment

7. When a conference or a group discussion is tending to turn into a *bull session* without constructive purpose, the BEST action to take is to

   A. reprimand the leader of the *bull session*
   B. redirect the discussion to the business at hand
   C. dismiss the meeting and reschedule it for another day
   D. allow the *bull session* to continue

8. Assume that you have been assigned responsibility for the overhaul program of the master controller on the R-32 cars in which a high production rate is mandatory. From past experience, you know that your foremen do not perform equally well in the various types of jobs given to them. Which of the following methods should you use in selecting foremen for the specific types of work involved in the overhaul program?

   A. Leave the method of selecting foremen to your supervisor
   B. Assign each foreman to the work he does best
   C. Allow each foreman to choose his own job
   D. Assign each foreman to a job which will permit him to improve his own abilities

9. Which one of the following is the PRIMARY objective in drawing up a set of specifications for materials to be purchased?

   A. Establishment of standard sizes
   B. Outline of intended use
   C. Method of inspection
   D. Control of quality

10. In the subway system, a major distinction between the cars of the A Division and of the B Division is that the _____ Division cars _____.

    A. B; cannot operate on the A Division
    B. A; cannot operate on the B Division
    C. B; are shorter than the A Division cars
    D. A; are higher than the B Division cars

11. Of the following, the MOST important function of an assistant supervisor is to

    A. write pertinent reports to his supervisor
    B. answer technical questions from his foremen
    C. delegate critical responsibilities to his foremen
    D. supervise in an efficient manner

12. Assume that you have determined that the work of one of your foremen and the men he supervises is consistently behind schedule. When you discuss this situation with the foreman, he tells you that his men are poor workers and then complains that he must spend all of his time checking on their work.
    The following actions are offered for your consideration as possible ways of solving the problem of poor performance of the foreman and his men:
    I. Review the work standards with the foreman and determine whether they are reliable
    II. Tell the foreman that you will recommend him for the foreman's training course for retraining

III. Ask the foreman for the names of the maintainers and then replace them as soon as possible
IV. Tell the foreman that you expect him to meet a satisfactory level of performance
V. Tell the foreman to insist that his men work overtime to catch up to the schedule
VI. Tell the foreman to review the type and amount of training he has given the maintainers
VII. Tell the foreman that he will be out of a job if he does not produce on schedule
VIII. Avoid all criticism of the foreman and his methods

Which of the following suggested answers CORRECTLY lists the proper actions to be taken to solve the problem of poor performance of the foreman and his men?

A. I, II, IV, VI
B. I, III, V, VII
C. II, III, VI, VIII
D. IV, V, VI, VIII

13. Assume that one of the foremen in a training course, which you are conducting, proposes a poor solution for a maintenance problem.
Of the following, the BEST course of action for you to take is to

A. accept the solution tentatively, and correct it during the next class meeting
B. point out all the defects of this proposed solution and wait until somebody thinks of a better solution
C. try to get the class to reject this proposed solution and develop a better solution
D. let the matter pass since somebody will present a better solution as the class work proceeds

14. While making a walking tour of the wheel shop, you observe a maintainer who is operating a hoisting system, replacing a sling which will be used to lift heavily laden pallets. The new sling which will now be used is identical to the old sling in construction except that the wire ropes are longer. The maintainer finds that the angle which the legs of the sling make with the horizontal changed from 45° on the old sling to 60° on the new sling. The following are possible changes in capability of the hoisting system directly resulting from the new sling.
The following are possible changes in capability of the hoisting system directly resulting from the new sling.
   I. The load carrying capability of the sling has been increased.
   II. The load carrying capability of the overhead hoist has been increased.
   III. The load carrying capability of the sling has been decreased.
   IV. The maximum clearance between the pallet and the shop floor has been decreased.

Which of the following suggested answers CORRECTLY describes the changes in the capability of the hoisting system directly resulting from the increased angle of the legs of the sling with the horizontal?

A. I, II
B. III only
C. I, IV
D. I, II, IV

15. In the R-44 car, the dynamic brake feedback sends a signal to a particular unit which eliminates the pneumatic brake operation until the speed of the train is approximately 10 MPH or less.
    The name of this unit is

    A. GR-90 tread brake unit
    B. A-13 electronic operating unit
    C. G-4B pneumatic operating unit
    D. J-relay valve

16. In statistical reports on shop injuries, the expression which describes a work injury resulting in death, permanent total disability, permanent partial disability, or temporary total disability is a

    A. medical treatment injury
    B. disabling injury
    C. disabling injury severity rate
    D. disabling injury frequency rate

17. The MAJOR components in the R-44 car RT 5C brake equipment are the _____ compressor, A-13 electronic unit, _____ pneumatic unit, and _____ brake unit.

    A. D-3; G4B; GR-90   B. D-3; G4B; ME-23
    C. A-1; G4B; GR-90   D. A-1; J; GR-90

18. In the R-44 car, an A-13 electronic operating unit is used to convert increasing or decreasing current level in the P-wire to an electrical request to the pneumatic operating unit for decreasing or increasing the brake cylinder pressure.
    The condition that must exist to terminate the change in pressure in the brake cylinder is that the feedback signal from the

    A. dynamic brake request is 1 milliamp (DC) less than the P-wire request
    B. dynamic brake request matches the P-wire request
    C. pneumatic operating unit matches the P-wire request
    D. pneumatic operating unit is 1 milliamp (DC) more than the P-wire request

Questions 19-21.

DIRECTIONS: When answering Questions 19 through 21, refer to the ACCIDENT CODE CLASSIFICATION listed below. The code lists letters that identify the responsibility for an accident and numbers that identify the cause of an accident. In answering the questions, select both the appropriate letter and number that classifies the accident described in the question, such as A-1, B-2, etc.

6 (#1)

ACCIDENT CODE CLASSIFICATION

Responsibility

A. Supervision

B. Employee

C. Other Employee

D. Impractical to control

E. Control of other than company or employee

Cause of Accident

1. Poor housekeeping

2. Defective construction, equipment, design

3. Tools, equipment (improper use or handling)

4. Protective equipment not provided

5. Protective equipment not used

6. Improper or inadequate instructions

7. Inattention

8. Failure to observe rules or orders

19. A maintainer suffers an eye injury while drilling holes in a casting. Investigation revealed that he was not wearing the approved type of safety glasses.
The classification for this injury should be

   A. A-4   B. A-6   C. B-4   D. B-5

20. A maintainer working near an open pit normally equipped with a removable guard rail falls into the pit and suffers head wounds.
The classification for this accident should be

   A. A-4   B. A-7   C. B-4   D. B-7

21. A maintainer working at his regular station suffers eye burns as a result of welding work being done on an air tank located about 10 feet from the maintainer's work station.
The classification of this injury should be

   A. A-2   B. A-4   C. B-5   D. B-7

22. It has been found necessary to remove a component from a printed circuit card used on an R-44 car.
Before the component can be removed, it is NECESSARY to

   A. remove the plastic coating from the card
   B. clean the card in an ultrasonic cleaning bath
   C. unsolder the multi-pin connector
   D. connect all capacitors on the card to a common ground

23. Of the following, the statement concerning hydraulic lifting jacks which is MOST appropriate is that, in general, the working fluid will   23._____

    A. not increase in temperature when loaded
    B. not change its viscosity when loaded
    C. increase in volume when loaded
    D. not freeze at a temperature of 32 ° F

24. A car wheel should be pressed on a truck axle with a force that is between _____ and   24._____
    _____ tons.

    A. 24; 38   B. 42; 53   C. 68; 90   D. 100; 142

25. The reporting card which should be used for recording the serial number of an air compressor installed on a subway car during overhaul is the   25._____

    A. individual car case history report
    B. road car inspector report
    C. R-10 and up cars-inspection card
    D. repair card, car level

KEY (CORRECT ANSWERS)

1.	C	11.	D
2.	B	12.	A
3.	A	13.	C
4.	D	14.	C
5.	C	15.	B
6.	B	16.	B
7.	B	17.	A
8.	B	18.	C
9.	D	19.	D
10.	A	20.	D

21. B
22. A
23. D
24. C
25. D

TEST 2

DIRECTIONS: Each question or incomplete statement is followed by several suggested answers or completions. Select the one that BEST answers the question or completes the statement. *PRINT THE LETTER OF THE CORRECT ANSWER IN THE SPACE AT THE RIGHT.*

1. The maintenance of subway cars is a continuing process. As a supervisor, you should be seeking ways to improve the efficiency of shop operations by means such as changing established work procedures.
   The following are offered as possible actions that you should consider in changing established work procedures.

   I. Make changes only when your foremen agree to them
   II. Discuss changes with your supervisor before putting them into practice
   III. Standardize any operation which is performed on a continuing basis
   IV. Make changes quickly and quietly in order to avoid dissent
   V. Secure expert guidance before instituting unfamiliar procedures

   Of the following suggested answers, the one that describes the actions to be taken to change established work procedures is

   A. I, IV, V
   B. II, III, V
   C. III, IV, V
   D. I, II, III, IV, V

   1.____

2. If a pair of channels are to be welded together to form a built-up beam, the arrangement which will produce the greatest transverse load carrying capacity is shown by the following cross section:

   2.____

   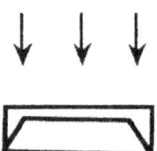 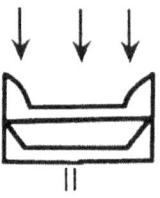 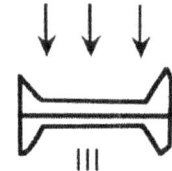 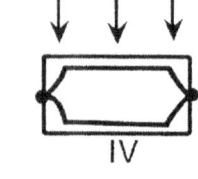

   A. I   B. II   C. III   D. IV

3. The CHIEF advantage of a differential chain hoist over an ordinary block and tackle is that

   A. a load suspended from a chain hoist will remain stationary without attention
   B. heavier loads can be lifted with a chain hoist than with a block and tackle
   C. loads can be raised more rapidly with a chain hoist than with a block and tackle
   D. the chain hoist costs less than the block and tackle

   3.____

4. In a work gang using a power hoist lift, it is the generally accepted practice that only one man in the group gives the signals to the operator of the hoist. There is, however, one exception.
   In this exception, any one of the group is permitted to give the _____ signal.

   A. boom-up   B. hoist   C. swing   D. stop

   4.____

5. A supervisor determined that a foreman, without informing his superior, delegated responsibility for checking time cards to a member of his gang. The supervisor then called the foreman into his office where he reprimanded the foreman.
   This action of the supervisor in reprimanding the foreman was

   A. *proper,* because the checking of time cards is the foreman's responsibility and should not be delegated
   B. *proper,* because the foreman did not ask the supervisor for permission to delegate responsibility
   C. *improper,* because the foreman may no longer take the initiative in solving future problems
   D. *improper,* because the supervisor is interfering in a function which is not his responsibility

5.____

6. After completing the silver brazing of a joint with an oxyacetylene torch, the maintainer should remove the residual flux and oxide by

   A. dipping the joint in hot oil
   B. washing the joint with hot water
   C. dipping the joint in sulphuric acid
   D. grinding the joint

6.____

7. The air-conditioning system on the R-42 subway cars can be described as having

   A. two independent refrigeration units, each of 9-ton capacity
   B. one refrigeration unit of 18-ton capacity
   C. two independent refrigeration units, each of 15-ton capacity
   D. one refrigeration unit of 30-ton capacity

7.____

8. When using an oxyacetylene torch to cut steel, the flame should contain

   A. an excess amount of acetylene
   B. an excess amount of oxygen
   C. equal amounts of acetylene and oxygen
   D. only acetylene

8.____

Questions 9-11.

DIRECTIONS: The following Questions 9 through 11, inclusive, refer to the information contained in the equipment code book of the cars and shop department. In this book, car equipment defects are identified with code numbers.

9. The code number that identifies the defect of *low refrigerant* in the air conditioning system is

   A. 180   B. 198   C. 209   D. 308

9.____

10. The code number that identifies the defect in a car with a flat spot $1\frac{1}{2}$ to $2\frac{1}{2}$ inches long is

    A. 100   B. 181   C. 199   D. 213

10.____

11. The code number indicating that no defect was found on the reported *low air pressure* on a trouble car is

    A. 011   B. 041   C. 136   D. 168

12. The master controller should NOT be held in the *switching* position for a prolonged period of time because, if held in this position, the

    A. compressed air needed for braking may be wasted
    B. air brakes may be automatically actuated
    C. starting resistors may burn out
    D. train may accelerate too rapidly

13. Of the following, the conditions which BEST describe the possible causes of an emergency brake application are a(n)

    A. open conductor's valve, a brake handle in *emergency,* or a blown compressor fuse
    B. brake handle in *emergency,* a blown compressor fuse, or a broken brake pipe
    C. blown compressor fuse, a broken brake pipe, or an open conductor's valve
    D. broken brake pipe, an open conductor's valve, or a brake handle in *emergency*

14. Which of the following fuses should a maintainer remove *before* he attempts to adjust the clearance between the pendulum contacts on the electric self-lapping portion of the ME 42B and ME 43 brake valves?

    A. ME 2   B. L 2   C. P 2   D. B 2

15. A road car inspector reports that the motorman's indication is dim.
    Of the following, the *probable* cause is that the

    A. batteries are weak
    B. air pressure is too high
    C. third rail voltage is too low
    D. air pressure is too low

16. Two yellow lanterns adjacent to the track indicate that

    A. a train is stalled
    B. men are working on the tracks
    C. a section of the subway is flooded
    D. power has been removed from a section of the third rail

17. The transit authority uses General Motors diesel engines on the crane cars.
    The starting of this engine by a maintainer with liquid fuel oil in the combustion chamber is considered

    A. *good* practice, because it makes starting easier
    B. *good* practice, because it decreases fuel oil consumption rate
    C. *poor* practice, because it increases fuel oil consumption rate
    D. *poor* practice, because it could cause physical damage to the engine

4 (#2)

18. A maintainer earns $18.66 per hour, and time and one-half for overtime over 40 hours. Each week, 15 percent of his total salary is deducted for social security and taxes. Also, each week a $27.00 deduction is made for a savings bond, and a $13.50 deduction is made for a charitable organization.
If he works a total of 46 hours in a week, his take-home pay for that week is

   A. $914.34   B. $777.15   C. $736.68   D. $616.05

18.____

19. A one-inch steel plate shown in the sketch at the right is to be used as part of a steel weldment. The weight of this plate is MOST NEARLY _____ pounds.

   A. 2,820
   B. 5,760
   C. 23,700
   D. 34,000

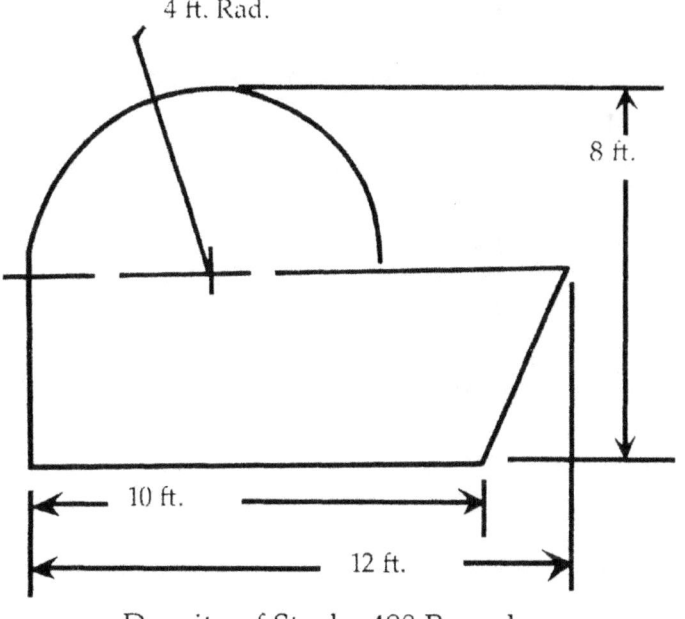

Density of Steel = 490 Pounds per Cu. Ft.

19.____

20. The refrigerant used in the R-42 air conditioning system is

   A. sulphur dioxide   B. Refrigerant-12
   C. Refrigerant-22   D. ammonia

20.____

21. In the R-44 subway car, the condensers of the air conditioning system are mounted

   A. under the car
   B. in a vertical cabinet at the No. 1 end of the A car
   C. in a false ceiling at the No. 1 end of each car
   D. in a false ceiling at the No. 2 end of each car

21.____

22. In a compression type air conditioning system, the refrigerant absorbs heat from the circulating air in the

   A. compressor   B. condenser
   C. evaporator   D. expansion valve

22.____

23. In the R-42 air conditioning system, non-cleanable type strainers are installed in the refrigerant liquid line in front of the evaporator.
To replace the strainers, it is NECESSARY to transfer the refrigerant charge to the

   A. compressor sump   B. evaporator
   C. condenser   D. receiver

23.____

24. The SMEE brake equipment uses a 3-YC air compressor which has two stages of compression.
Air is admitted into the *first* stage by the action of the

    A. compressor camshaft opening the intake poppet valves
    B. compressor crankshaft opening the intake valves
    C. second stage discharge pressure opening the intake disc valves
    D. partial vacuum created by the downward stroke of the first stage piston opening the intake disc valves

25. Which of the following symbols should you expect to find on a circuit diagram of a printed circuit card?

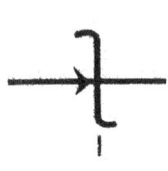 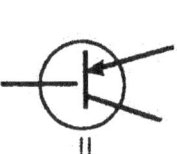  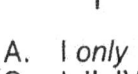

    A. I only
    B. I, III
    C. I, II, IV
    D. I, II, III, IV

KEY (CORRECT ANSWERS)

1.	B	11.	A
2.	D	12.	C
3.	A	13.	D
4.	D	14.	D
5.	A	15.	A
6.	B	16.	B
7.	A	17.	D
8.	B	18.	C
9.	D	19.	A
10.	B	20.	C

21. A
22. C
23. D
24. D
25. C

TEST 3

DIRECTIONS: Each question or incomplete statement is followed by several suggested answers or completions. Select the one that BEST answers the question or completes the statement. *PRINT THE LETTER OF THE CORRECT ANSWER IN THE SPACE AT THE RIGHT.*

1. An *inshot valve* is used on subway cars furnished with the SMEE brake equipment. The following statements are offered for your consideration as possibly applying to the *inshot valve*.
   It

   I. provides sufficient air to the brake cylinders to place the brake shoes against the car wheels while the dynamic brake is applied
   II. provides sufficient air to the brake cylinders to place the brake shoes against the car wheels while the pneumatic brake is applied
   III. supplies supplementary air to the brakes when the car loading requires braking effort in excess of the dynamic brake capacity
   IV. supplies control air to regulate the operation of the variable load valves

   Of the following suggested answers, the one which applies to the *inshot valve* is

   A. I only   B. II only   C. I, III   D. I, IV

1.____

2. A supervisor while walking through the shop notices a maintainer soldering a transistor to a printed circuit card with a 150-watt soldering iron.
   This is a

   A. *good* practice, because it increases production
   B. *good* practice, because it will make a strong joint of high conductivity
   C. *poor* practice, because it may decrease the insulation resistance of the card
   D. *poor* practice, because it may damage the transistor

2.____

3. An R-44 car is brought into the shop with the complaint that the *brake pipe fails to charge*.
   The following items are offered for your consideration as causes of this reported defect.

   I. Defective recharge magnet valve
   II. Brake pipe rupture on the car body
   III. Brake pipe rupture at the draw bar
   IV. Brake pipe rupture on the head operating car

   Of the following suggested answers, the one which describes the CAUSE of the reported defect is

   A. I *only*   B. I, II
   C. I, II, III   D. I, II, III, IV

3.____

Questions 4-9.

DIRECTIONS: Questions 4 through 9 are based on the drawing of the SPINDLE SHAFT shown below. Consult this drawing when answering these questions.

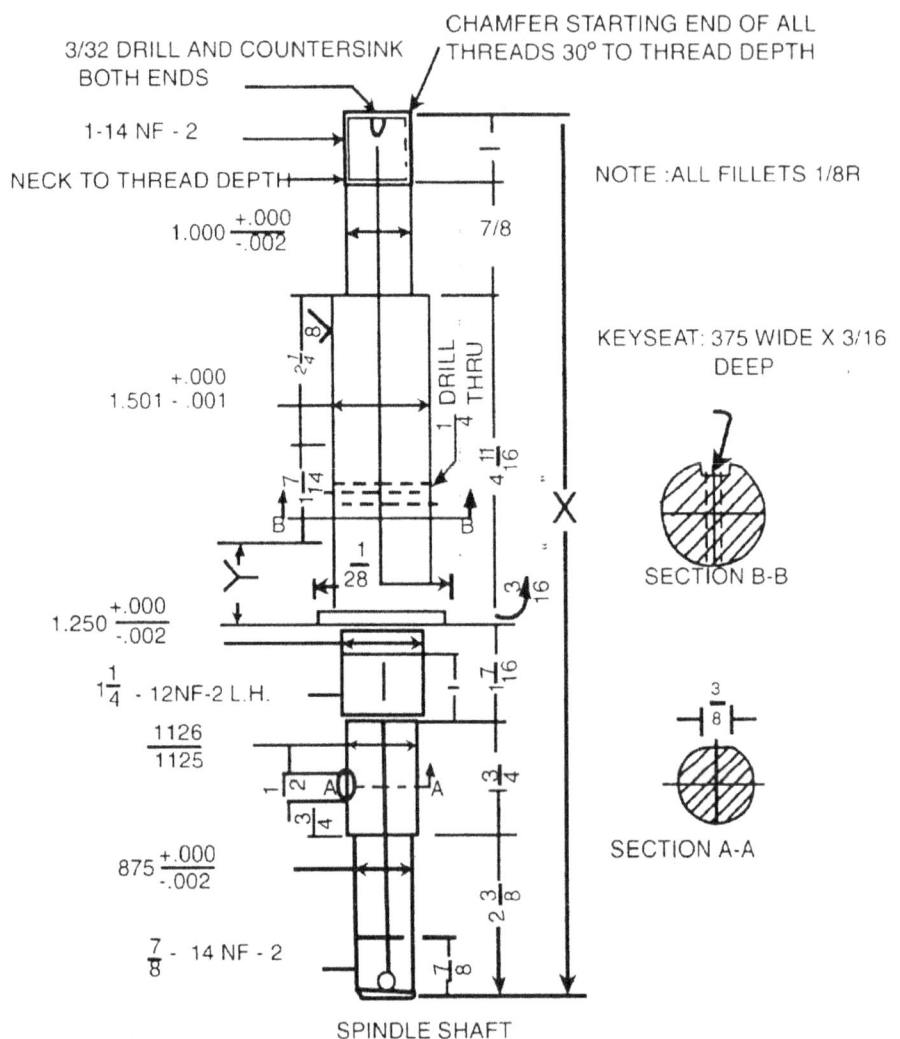

SPINDLE SHAFT

Material - Nickel - Chrome Steel 4140
Brinnell - 290
All dimensions in inches
Machine finish 125 all over except as noted

4. The dimensions of the steel stock from which the shaft would *probably* be machined are _____ dia. x _____ lg.

 A. $1\frac{1}{2}"$; 13"   B. 2"; 14"   C. $2\frac{1}{4}"$; 14"   D. $2\frac{1}{2}"$; 13"

5. The number 14 in the expression 7/8-14NF-2 represents the

 A. outside diameter in millimeters
 B. pitch diameter in millimeters
 C. number of threads per inch
 D. surface roughness in microinches

6. A bronze sleeve having an I.D. of .998-.996" is to be shrunk onto the 1.000" .998" diameter portion of the shaft.
   The MAXIMUM interference between sleeve and shaft is

   A. .001"   B. .002"   C. .003"   D. .004"

7. The machine tool that would *probably* be used to obtain
   1.501 $^{+.000}_{.001}$ diameter of the shaft is a

   A. shaper   B. planer
   C. lathe   D. cutting machine

8. The expression *Brinell-290"* indicates the

   A. type of steel used
   B. hardness of the steel
   C. tensile strength of the material
   D. density of the material

9. The *nominal* size of the square key that should be used with this shaft is _____ inch.

   A. 3/16   B. 3/8   C. 1/2   D. 1 7/16

10. In the car maintenance department, the function of analyzing and reporting train trouble is a responsibility of the _____ section.

    A. operations
    B. quality control
    C. maintenance, planning, and engineering
    D. material control

11. In the car maintenance department, the function of determining car problem areas and of developing associated corrective actions is a responsibility of the

    A. operations section
    B. quality control section
    C. maintenance, planning, and engineering section
    D. repair shop

12. The transit authority has conducted studies on the performance of fluorescent tube lights in subway cars. One of the factors studied was the effect of power interruptions caused by the contact shoes going over the third rail gaps. The following possible effects resulting from power interruptions are offered for your consideration.
    The
    I. life of tube lights is increased
    II. life of tube lights is decreased
    III. brightness of tube lights is doubled
    IV. brightness of tube lights is increased for short intervals of time
    Of the following suggested answers, the one which describes the effects resulting from power interruptions is

    A. I *only*   B. II *only*   C. II, III   D. I, IV

13. The R-44 car has two types of circuit breakers, designated as the high voltage and the low voltage circuit breakers. On the B car, the low voltage circuit breakers are located at the No. 1 end of the B side of the car and the high voltage circuit breakers are located at the _____ side(s) of the car.

   A. No. 2 end of the A
   B. No. 2 end of the B
   C. No. 1 end on the A
   D. No. 1 end on both the A and B

14. A car should be stopped if the flange thickness of a wheel on this car as determined with a No. 230 gage is equal to or _____ than _____ inch(es).

   A. more; $1\frac{1}{4}$
   B. more; 1 1/8
   C. more; 1
   D. less; 15/16

15. A supervisor is informed that a truck cannot be released if the wheels on a truck-axle assembly of the truck differ by 1/8" or more in diameter.
   If the circumference of one wheel on a truck assembly which is used as a reference wheel measures 97 3/4 inches, then the *limiting* dimensions of the other wheel circumference are _____ to _____ inches.

   A. 97 1/64; 97 41/64
   B. 97 17/64; 97 57/64
   C. 97 23/64; 98 9/64
   D. 97 39/64; 98 25/64

16. The office of the superintendent of transportation must be notified when a group of maintainers is scheduled to work under flagging protection at a given track location. The notification is NECESSARY in order to

   A. permit reducing the number of runs on the track
   B. alert the motormen operating on the track that maintainers are at work
   C. permit notifying passengers of possible delays
   D. facilitate delivery of materials required by the maintainers

17. The following are duties of the quality control section in the car maintenance department. The following possible duties are offered for your consideration.
   I. Sets procedures for the inspection and repair of car equipment
   II. Insures accepted level of performance in car repairs
   III. Analyzes and adjusts signal system failures
   IV. Investigates and approves new car equipment
   V. Conducts research and development on car equipment
   VI. Insures maintenance of production quotas in car repairs
   VII. Monitors savings due to reduction in overtime

   Which of the following suggested answers describes the duties of the quality control section?

   A. I, II, III
   B. I, II, III, IV
   C. I, II, IV, V
   D. I, II, III, VI, VII

18. When the thermal switch on an R-44 door operator motor is open, the door will   18.____
    A. remain closed at all times
    B. remain open at all times
    C. operate at a speed slower than normal
    D. operate at a speed faster than normal

19. For you to fulfill the duties and responsibilities which are inherent in your position and in   19.____
    order to gain the full approval of your superior, there are certain basic essentials that you
    must master.
    The following are offered for your consideration as being possible essentials which you
    should master in order to relate effectively to your superior.
    Understanding
        I.   your duties and assuming your responsibilities
        II. the needs of your superior for information feedback from you
        III. the preferences of your superior
        IV. the desire of your superior to be friendly with you
    Of the following suggested answers, the one which describes the ESSENTIALS that
    should be mastered is

    A. I only   B. II only
    C. I, IV   D. I, II, III

20. Diesel-engine operated locomotives in the transit system are used PRIMARILY for the   20.____
    A. inspection of track conditions
    B. removal of snow
    C. moving of trains in and out of the inspection barns
    D. work trains in the maintenance of way department

21. The coupler electric portion contact carrier provides a means whereby the control cable 21.____
    of one car may be readily connected to that of another car.
    The following devices are offered for your consideration as being possibly controlled
    through the coupler electric portion contact carrier.
        I.   Traction motor
        II. Door control
        III. Electro-pneumatic brake control
        IV. Fan and heater control
        V.   Interior light control
    Of the following suggested answers, the one that identifies the devices controlled
    through the electric coupler portion is

    A. I, II   B. II, III
    C. II, III, IV   D. I, II, III, IV, V

22. The M-3-A lead valve used on the SMEE equipment is preset to automatically maintain a   22.____
    pressure of _____ psi.

    A. 85   B. 95   C. 110   D. 125

23. The ME-23 brake valve is used on cars provided with the   23.____

    A. UE-5 brake equipment   B. M-3-A feed valve
    C. A-1 operating unit   D. A-3 compressor unit

24. The derailment-collision committee consists of designated members of the following departments: maintenance of way (track and signal), car maintenance, transportation, engineering, and

   A. station   B. power   C. legal   D. safety

25. Subway cars are equipped with air compressors to operate the pneumatic equipment. The moisture in the compressed air is condensed in the compressor reservoir and is discharged

   A. by the road car inspector periodically by opening the drain valve
   B. by the motorman at the terminal before the start of the run
   C. automatically with each operating cycle of the compressor governor
   D. automatically as a vapor with the use of a high voltage heating coil

26. On the R-10 to R-40 type cars, the motors of the electric door operators are supplied with

   A. 32 volts DC   B. 115 volts AC
   C. 300 volts DC   D. 600 volts DC

Questions 27-28.

DIRECTIONS: Questions 27 and 28 are based on the following paragraph.

The car maintenance department is considering the purchase of a certain car part from Manufacturer X for $210. An equivalent part can be purchased from Manufacturer Y for $150. The part made by Manufacturer X must be reconditioned every 3 years using material that costs $45 and requires 6 hours of labor. The part made by Manufacturer Y must be reconditioned every 1 1/2 years using material that costs $36 and requires 5 hours of labor. The maintainer's rate of pay is $18 per hour.

27. The cost of operating with the part made by Manufacturer X (excluding the first cost) is MOST NEARLY _____ per year.

   A. $45   B. $48   C. $51   D. $63

28. The total cost of operating with the part made by Manufacturer Y over a period of 12 years, including the first cost of the part and assuming the part is scrapped at the end of 12 years, is MOST NEARLY

   A. $708   B. $858   C. $1,032   D. $1,158

29. You have been requested by your superior to investigate the cause of the poor finish and out of tolerance condition of the wheels machined on the wheel truing machine in the shop. You are told that this is an urgent job and that a written report is desired giving the correct actions to be taken to solve the problem.
    The following characteristics of a written report which would be of greatest value to your superior are offered for your consideration.
    I. Detailed description of the problem
    II. Brief description of the problem
    III. Descriptions of possible solutions
    IV. Recommended corrective actions
    V. Detailed sketches of the wheels and of the wheel truing machine

Of the following suggested answers, the one that describes a report of GREATEST value to your superior is

    A. I, III
    B. II, IV
    C. I, III, IV
    D. I, III, IV, V

30. The Atlas Crane cars use General Motors 6-cylinder, V-type, 2-stroke cycle engines. One of these engines is operating with a low air box pressure resulting in inefficient combustion and scavenging.
The following faults are offered for your consideration as being possibly responsible for the low air box pressure.
    I. High air inlet restrictions
    II. Damaged blower rotors
    III. Clogged blower air inlet screen
    IV. High exhaust back pressure
Of the following suggested answers, the one that describes the CAUSES of the low air box pressure is

    A. I, II
    B. I, II, III
    C. I, II, IV
    D. II, III, IV

KEY (CORRECT ANSWERS)

1.	C	16.	B
2.	D	17.	C
3.	D	18.	C
4.	C	19.	D
5.	C	20.	D
6.	D	21.	D
7.	C	22.	C
8.	B	23.	A
9.	B	24.	D
10.	C	25.	C
11.	B	26.	A
12.	B	27.	C
13.	C	28.	C
14.	D	29.	B
15.	C	30.	B

EXAMINATION SECTION
TEST 1

DIRECTIONS: Each question or incomplete statement is followed by several suggested answers or completions. Select the one that BEST answers the question or completes the statement. *PRINT THE LETTER OF THE CORRECT ANSWER IN THE SPACE AT THE RIGHT.*

1. On R-10 cars, the number of conductor's master door control switches on each car is

    A. 7   B. 6   C. 5   D. 4

2. The electric door operator toggle switch for cutting out a door is located

    A. in No. 1 cab
    B. in No. 2 cab
    C. under a seat cushion
    D. on No. 1 panel board

3. In cars of the R-9 type, excessive brake shoe clearance would MOST likely result in

    A. a poor brake application
    B. undertravel of the brake cylinder slack adjuster
    C. excessive brake shoe wear
    D. dragging brakes

4. A car wheel tread is usually checked for wear with a _____ gage.

    A. surface
    B. contour
    C. depth
    D. micrometer

5. To remove power from a subway car, the number of contact shoes which must be slippered is

    A. 5   B. 2   C. 6   D. 7

6. On the newer subway cars, a change in the center plate has made it UNNECESSARY to use

    A. king pins
    B. drawbar pins
    C. yoke pins
    D. swing links

7. To remove a journal brass, it is NECESSARY to use a jack under the car

    A. bolster
    B. side frame
    C. end frame
    D. journal box

8. On a subway car truck, a defective dust guard may cause injury to the

    A. transom
    B. side bearing
    C. journal bearing
    D. center casting

9. The self-closing of a car end door is accomplished by means of a closing device based on the use of a(n)

    A. compression spring
    B. air cylinder
    C. tension spring
    D. counterweight

10. Brake rigging slack which is NOT corrected by the slack adjuster is MOST likely to result in

A. slower braking
B. faster braking
C. binding brakes
D. excessive brake rigging wear

11. If there is no air pressure on a pneumatically operated door engine, but the electrical circuits are OK, then the   11.____

    A. door will be inoperative
    B. motorman's indication light will fail to work properly
    C. door can still be operated electrically
    D. conductor's signal light will fail to work properly

12. The truck bolster rests DIRECTLY on the   12.____

    A. swing hangers   B. center casting
    C. bolster springs   D. spring plank

13. Excessive car swaying would MOST likely be caused by   13.____

    A. worn side bearings
    B. excessive truck frame camber
    C. insufficient journal bearing clearance
    D. incorrect adjustment of height adjuster

14. Car body height is GENERALLY measured from the top of the rail to the Z   14.____

    A. top of the belt rail
    B. bottom of the anti-climber
    C. bottom of the center sill
    D. top of the anti-climber

15. When inspecting a truck coil spring, the IMPORTANT defect a car inspector should check for is   15.____

    A. tension   B. flexibility
    C. free height   D. compression

16. The TOTAL number of end door engines used on a car with 4 double leaf doors per side is   16.____

    A. 4   B. 5   C. 6   D. 7

17. A car inspector checking a truck need NOT inspect the   17.____

    A. drawbar carrier   B. equalizer bars
    C. pedestal casting   D. spring plank

18. A car inspector checking a truck would NOT have to inspect the   18.____

    A. pedestal casting   B. drawbar carrier
    C. equalizer bars   D. swing hangers

19. Elastic stop nuts are MOST generally used on _____ screws.   19.____

    A. self-tapping   B. machine
    C. lag   D. wood

20. The TOTAL number of brake cylinders on a car of the R-10 type is 20._____

    A. 7   B. 6   C. 5   D. 4

KEY (CORRECT ANSWERS)

1. D
2. C
3. A
4. B
5. B

6. A
7. D
8. C
9. D
10. A

11. A
12. C
13. A
14. D
15. D

16. B
17. A
18. B
19. B
20. D

TEST 2

DIRECTIONS: Each question or incomplete statement is followed by several suggested answers or completions. Select the one that BEST answers the question or completes the statement. *PRINT THE LETTER OF THE CORRECT ANSWER IN THE SPACE AT THE RIGHT.*

1. If a car inspector finds a subway car contact shoe is low, he SHOULD

    A. put in two new pivots
    B. replace wear pad key
    C. simply adjust shoe to its proper height
    D. condemn the shoe and replace it

2. Of the following defects, the MOST serious is a

    A. cracked axle   B. sagged elliptic spring
    C. wheel flat spot   D. hot journal

3. If a car inspector finds a train in passenger service that has a car with a missing brake shoe, the MAIN thing he should do is

    A. remove the brake shoe hanger for this shoe
    B. immediately install a new shoe in place of the missing shoe
    C. tie up the brake rigging on this car
    D. cut out the brakes on this car

4. The coupler is DIRECTLY connected to the

    A. truck bolster   B. car body underframe
    C. drawbar   D. car body bolster

5. Normal wheel wear is compensated for by the adjustment of the

    A. brake shoe slack adjuster
    B. journal bearing wedge
    C. brake cylinder slack adjuster
    D. bolster height adjuster

6. A thermal cutout is used on the newer cars to protect the

    A. slack adjusters   B. side bearings
    C. door engines   D. journal bearings

7. If a car inspector finds a coupler is low, he SHOULD

    A. install a new coupler head
    B. simply adjust the coupler to its proper height
    C. shim up the yoke
    D. lubricate the drawbar

8. A wear plate is used on the

    A. drawbar carrier   B. end sills
    C. shoe beam   D. motor gears

9. The TOTAL number of door engines used on an R-17 car, which has three double leaf doors per side, is

   A. 11 B. 9 C. 8 D. 7

9._____

10. A thermal cut-out is used on the

    A. pneumatic door operators
    B. fluorescent lights
    C. electric door operators
    D. electric brake

10._____

11. The guard lights indicate

    A. if power is on the traction motors
    B. if power is on the electric door operators
    C. whether the side doors are opened
    D. if the electric brake is operative

11._____

12. The dry chemical fire extinguisher is PREFERABLE to the carbon tetrachloride extinguisher mainly because it is

    A. less expensive
    B. less toxic
    C. more compact
    D. not as heavy

12._____

13. The center sills are a part of the car

    A. underframe
    B. truck
    C. roof
    D. draft gear

13._____

14. The MOST likely cause for the dropping of a brake shoe from a car in passenger service would be a

    A. defective slack adjuster
    B. broken brake shoe key
    C. defective brake cylinder
    D. worn wheel

14._____

15. A swing panel is used to gain access to the

    A. heaters
    B. cut-out cocks
    C. door pockets
    D. motor gears

15._____

16. Shoe beams should be kept free of steel dust MAINLY to avoid

    A. electrolysis
    B. corrosion
    C. electrical breakdown
    D. rotting

16._____

17. New cars have shock absorbers on the trucks. These are used MAINLY to

    A. reduce wheel wear
    B. protect the car axles
    C. reduce journal bearing wear
    D. reduce vertical and lateral motion

17._____

18. Marks indicating rubbing on a side door panel would MOST likely be caused by a

    A. bent door lever
    B. bent floor plate

18._____

C. stuck magnet valve
D. seized motor operator

19. The brake shoes are secured in place with a

    A. king pin
    B. clasp
    C. key
    D. carrier pin

20. A car inspector could MOST easily check car body rivets for tightness by

    A. fluoroscope inspection
    B. testing with a pair of feelers
    C. sound detection with a hammer
    D. painting with whiting

KEY (CORRECT ANSWERS)

1. C	11. C
2. A	12. B
3. D	13. A
4. C	14. B
5. D	15. C
6. C	16. C
7. B	17. D
8. A	18. A
9. C	19. C
10. C	20. C

TEST 3

DIRECTIONS: Each question or incomplete statement is followed by several suggested answers or completions. Select the one that BEST answers the question or completes the statement. *PRINT THE LETTER OF THE CORRECT ANSWER IN THE SPACE AT THE RIGHT.*

1. The wheels of a car truck may wear sufficiently to require a readjustment at the 1.____

   A. axle bearings
   B. transom
   C. spring plank
   D. bolster height adjuster

2. Brake rigging slack which is NOT corrected by the slack adjuster is MOST likely to result in 2.____

   A. binding brakes
   B. excessive brake rigging wear
   C. faster braking
   D. slower braking

3. The number of trip cocks on a subway car truck in passenger service is 3.____

   A. one B. two C. three D. four

4. Car wheels which are worn below the minimum wheel diameter and have sharp flanges would be 4.____

   A. scrapped
   B. turned down to remove the sharp flanges
   C. checked for eccentricity
   D. continued in service until the flanges wear down

5. Cotton waste should NOT be used to wipe journal bearings because it 5.____

   A. contains too many impurities
   B. is not sufficiently absorbent
   C. is too expensive
   D. may cause a waste grab

6. If a car inspector finds it necessary to make an emergency repair on the truck of a car in passenger service, he SHOULD 6.____

   A. pull out the shoe fuses
   B. wear rubber gloves while making the repair
   C. make sure power is off all four running tracks
   D. slipper the contact shoes of this car

7. At the conductor's operating position, the door control drum switch SHOULD be set to the _____ position. 7.____

   A. ON B. OFF C. THRU D. END

8. When inspecting the bolster coil springs on a truck, a car inspector SHOULD check for 8.____

   A. an elongated spring
   B. a stiff spring
   C. a weak spring
   D. free height

47

9. Losing a brake shoe on the road could MOST likely be caused by a

   A. worn brake shoe
   B. defective slack adjuster
   C. worn side bearing
   D. broken brake shoe key

10. A car inspector checking a truck need NOT inspect the

   A. equalizer bars   B. drawbar carrier
   C. spring plank   D. pedestal casting

11. A truck part which is NOT directly supported by the journal box is the

   A. shoe beam   B. trip cock
   C. equalizer bar   D. motor nose support

12. Normal wheel wear is compensated for by the adjustment of the

   A. bolster height adjuster
   B. brake cylinder slack adjuster
   C. journal bearing wedge
   D. brake shoe slack adjuster

13. Safety hangers are provided on the trucks for protection of the spring plank in case of the breaking of a(n)

   A. bolster spring   B. equalizer spring
   C. journal box   D. swing link

14. A bottom, side door track is a part of the

   A. threshold plate   B. side sill
   C. center sill   D. side plat

15. A POSSIBLE cause for a slow pneumatically operated door could be

   A. a defective master door controller
   B. excessive main reservoir pressure
   C. a partially clogged speed plug orifice
   D. a grounded synchronizing wire

16. On the newer cars, wheel wear has been reduced MAINLY through the use of

   A. journal bearings
   B. smaller wheels
   C. fewer brake cylinders per truck
   D. dynamic braking

17. A thermal cutout is used on the newer cars to protect the

   A. door engines   B. journal bearings
   C. side bearings   D. slack adjusters

18. Laminated glass is used in the front sash of the motor-man's cab MAINLY to

   A. reduce glare
   B. prevent reflections

C. provide protection from breakage
D. provide heat insulation

19. To ACCURATELY determine the tightness of a subway car trip cock, the device used is a   19._____

    A. torque wrench
    B. height gauge
    C. spring scale
    D. compression tester

20. Of the following, the metal which is MOST likely to crack when struck a heavy blow is   20._____

    A. forged steel
    B. cast iron
    C. wrought iron
    D. stainless steel

KEY (CORRECT ANSWERS)

1.	D	11.	D
2.	D	12.	A
3.	A	13.	D
4.	A	14.	A
5.	D	15.	C
6.	D	16.	D
7.	A	17.	A
8.	C	18.	C
9.	D	19.	C
10.	B	20.	B

TEST 4

DIRECTIONS: Each question or incomplete statement is followed by several suggested answers or completions. Select the one that BEST answers the question or completes the statement. *PRINT THE LETTER OF THE CORRECT ANSWER IN THE SPACE AT THE RIGHT.*

1. The self-closing of a car end door is accomplished by means of a closing device based on the use of a(n)   1._____

    A. tension spring
    B. compression spring
    C. counterweight
    D. air cylinder

2. Dragging brakes would NOT be the result of a   2._____

    A. leaking brake pipe
    B. blown compressor fuse
    C. hand brake partially set up
    D. broken pull rod

3. When a door engine thermal cutout on an R-17 subway car is tripped,   3._____

    A. the affected door will operate slowly
    B. the door will not operate
    C. air will be released from the closing cylinder
    D. it can be reset from the conductor's operating position

4. The MOST important reason for maintaining uniform brake piston travel is to attain   4._____

    A. longer life of parts
    B. quiet operation
    C. maximum braking effort
    D. equal braking

5. The emergency hand brake sheave is connected to the brake system by means of   5._____

    A. gears   B. chain   C. cable   D. levers

6. The truck bolster springs rest on the   6._____

    A. truck frame
    B. equalizer
    C. spring plank
    D. journal boxes

7. The swing links DIRECTLY support the   7._____

    A. bolster
    B. center casting
    C. spring plank
    D. pedestal casting

8. The total number of end door engines used on a car with 4 double leaf doors per side is   8._____

    A. 8   B. 6   C. 4   D. 2

9. Locked wheels on a subway car are LEAST likely to be the result of   9._____

    A. stuck brakes
    B. brakes cut out on a motor car
    C. traction motor gear trouble
    D. a dropped traction motor armature

10. Passengers would NOT be discharged from a train if one of the cars had a   10._____

A. broken truck frame
B. wheel with a 1/2" flat spot
C. broken equalizer bar
D. cracked axle

11. When a car inspector finds it necessary to work over or near a live third rail, then it is BEST to cover the third rail with a

   A. shoe paddle
   B. rubber mat
   C. large newspaper
   D. canvas cloth

11._____

12. If all the doors in a train cannot be opened, then a LIKELY trouble would be a(n)

   A. defective M.F. door relay
   B. open wire in the motorman's indication circuit
   C. jammed door engine
   D. broken door lock

12._____

13. A contour gauge would be used to check a subway car

   A. coil spring
   B. wheel
   C. bolster
   D. Woodward adjuster

13._____

14. The brake shoes are fastened in place with a

   A. key
   B. king pin
   C. carrier pin
   D. clasp

14._____

15. To remove a journal brass, it is necessary to FIRST

   A. jack up the journal box
   B. remove the pedestal binder
   C. insert a journal keeper
   D. jack up the car axle

15._____

16. If a car inspector finds a coupler is low, he should

   A. simply adjust the coupler to its proper height
   B. shim up the yoke
   C. install a new coupler head
   D. shop the car

16._____

17. Marks indicating rubbing on a side door panel would MOST likely be caused by a

   A. bent floor plate
   B. stuck magnet valve
   C. seized motor operator
   D. bent door lever

17._____

18. A subway car is reported for grooved or gouged wheels. A POSSIBLE cause for which a car Inspector should check is

   A. a bent shoe hanger
   B. worn wheel flanges
   C. worn side bearings
   D. a cracked safety hanger

18._____

19. Shoe beams should be kept free of brake shoe dust to avoid

   A. dry rotting
   B. electrical leakage
   C. warping
   D. moisture seepage

19._____

20. A car inspector checking a car reported for no brakes should inspect for 20._____

    A. a curved radius bar   B. excessive wheel wear
    C. closed cut-out cocks   D. worn wheel flanges

KEY(CORRECT ANSWERS)

1.	C	11.	B
2.	B	12.	A
3.	A	13.	B
4.	D	14.	A
5.	B	15.	A
6.	C	16.	A
7.	C	17.	D
8.	C	18.	A
9.	B	19.	B
10.	B	20.	C

EXAMINATION SECTION
TEST 1

DIRECTIONS: Each question or incomplete statement is followed by several suggested answers or completions. Select the one that BEST answers the question or completes the statement. *PRINT THE LETTER OF THE CORRECT ANSWER IN THE SPACE AT THE RIGHT.*

1. One indication that a car journal bearing had probably run hot would be

    A. oil dripping from the journal
    B. pieces of babbitt in the waste
    C. warm wheel treads
    D. a cracked wheel hub

    1._____

2. Lubrication is carried to a non-roller bearing surface in a journal box by the use of

    A. waste packing
    B. oil rings
    C. grooves in the shaft
    D. grooves in the bearing

    2._____

3. If one car of a married-pair in a train of 10 cars develops a grounded shoe beam, the NUMBER of hexagonal contact-shoe keys that must be knocked out by the car inspector if the train is to proceed without arcing and without broken contact shoe fuses is

    A. 2   B. 4   C. 6   D. 8

    3._____

4. A car inspector checking a truck would NOT have to inspect the

    A. swing hangers
    B. pedestal casting
    C. drawbar carrier
    D. equalizer springs

    4._____

5. A broken pawl on a married-pair car would prevent

    A. retrieving of the coupler electric portion
    B. application of the emergency brake
    C. application of the hand brake
    D. operation of the uncoupling valve

    5._____

6. A 7" x 6" brake cylinder has a 7"_____ and a 6" _____ .

    A. stroke; diameter
    B. diameter; stroke
    C. radius; stroke
    D. stroke; radius

    6._____

7. On R-9 and similar cars having only a single brake cylinder, air piping on trucks is LIMITED to that required for the

    A. brake pipe
    B. main air line
    C. variable load valve
    D. trip cocks

    7._____

8. The MAXIMUM radial misalignment of type H-2-C couplers that will still permit the couplers to *gather* and couple is _____ inches.

    A. 3   B. 4   C. 5   D. 8

    8._____

9. A car inspector can observe whether a slack adjuster is operative by having the

    A. reverser key moved from forward to reverse and back several times

    9._____

53

B. brakes repeatedly applied in emergency and then released
C. master controller placed in multiple with the control switch OFF
D. compressor switch alternately cut in and out

10. The contour gage is GENERALLY used to check the wear of

    A. journal brasses
    B. brake shoes
    C. wheel treads
    D. gear teeth

11. The center sills are structural members which extend from

    A. end to end of the car body
    B. side to side of the car body
    C. side to side of each truck
    D. end to end of each truck

12. Link bars are the mechanical couplers that are used for connecting-up the

    A. end sections to the middle section of the 3-section (type D) cars
    B. end cars to the middle car of the semi-permanently coupled (type A-B) units
    C. number two ends of married-pair cars
    D. flat cars on the open ends of work trains to the motor ears

13. Marks indicating rubbing on a side door panel would MOST likely be caused by a

    A. loose body rivet
    B. bent floor plate
    C. bent door lever
    D. loose glass frame

14. The FIRST step in cutting out a side door that is stuck open on a car in passenger service having electric door operators is to

    A. move the toggle switch to the OFF position
    B. pull the door panel or panels fully closed manually
    C. move the manual locking device to the LOCK position
    D. move the toggle switch to DOOR CUT-OUT position

15. The FIRST step in cutting out a side door that is stuck open on a car in passenger service having pneumatic door operators is to

    A. pull the door panel or panels fully closed manually
    B. move the toggle switch to the OFF position
    C. move the manual locking device to the LOCK position
    D. close the cut-out cock leading to the door engine

16. The NUMBER of door control drum switches that must be operated to change the keying of a 10-car train from 4-6 to 6-4 is

    A. 2   B. 4   C. 6   D. 8

17. Car body height is gauged from

    A. car floor to inside of roof
    B. base of rail to outside of roof
    C. top of rail to top of anti-telescoping plate
    D. tread of wheel to floor of car

18. Adjusting gibs are provided on trucks to adjust the position of 18.____

    A. spring planks
    B. contact shoe beams
    C. journal brasses
    D. bolster springs

19. The cause for the dropping of a brake shoe from a car in passenger service is MOST probably a broken 19.____

    A. live lever
    B. brake hanger
    C. clevis
    D. brake shoe key

20. Yokes and yoke pins are parts of the 20.____

    A. drawbar equipment
    B. bolster assemblies
    C. brake rigging
    D. spring plank suspensions

KEY (CORRECT ANSWERS)

1.	B	11.	A
2.	A	12.	C
3.	B	13.	C
4.	C	14.	A
5.	C	15.	D
6.	B	16.	B
7.	D	17.	C
8.	D	18.	B
9.	B	19.	D
10.	C	20.	A

TEST 2

DIRECTIONS: Each question or incomplete statement is followed by several suggested answers or completions. Select the one that BEST answers the question or completes the statement. *PRINT THE LETTER OF THE CORRECT ANSWER IN THE SPACE AT THE RIGHT.*

1. The coupler is DIRECTLY connected to the

    A. drawbar
    B. car body underframe
    C. car body bolster
    D. truck bolster

    1.____

2. Shoe beams should be kept free of brake shoe dust to avoid

    A. dry rotting
    B. electrical leakage
    C. warping
    D. moisture

    2.____

3. In the case of a major train trouble, it is a good policy for a road car inspector to ride the defective train to the terminal.
   A road car inspector should follow this policy in the case of a train with

    A. a worn journal bearing
    B. worn side bearings
    C. two side doors not working
    D. brake rigging which has fallen and which has been tied up

    3.____

4. The PROPER method of slowing down a side door which closes too rapidly is to

    A. change the ratio of the operating levers
    B. increase the resistance in the door magnet circuit
    C. decrease the battery voltage
    D. restrict the flow of air into the door engine cylinder

    4.____

5. At the conductor's operating position, the door control drum switch should be set to the _____ position.

    A. ON   B. OFF   C. THRU   D. END

    5.____

6. When inspecting the bolster coil springs on a truck, a road car inspector should check for

    A. an elongated spring
    B. a stiff spring
    C. a weak spring
    D. free height

    6.____

7. Badly worn car side bearing would tend to result in excessive

    A. eccentricity
    B. camber
    C. wheel pounding
    D. swaying

    7.____

8. A truck part which is NOT directly supported by the journal box is the

    A. shoe beam
    B. trip cock
    C. equalizer bar
    D. motor nose support

    8.____

9. Normal wheel wear is compensated for by the adjustment of the

    A. bolster height adjuster
    B. brake cylinder slack adjuster

    9.____

56

C. journal bearing wedge
D. brake shoe slack adjuster

10. The car part that must be dismantled before a traction motor can be removed from a truck is the

    A. pedestal binder
    B. transom plate
    C. spring plank
    D. axle caps

11. If a road car inspector finds that a car has one inoperative side door, a possible cause which he should check for is

    A. an obstruction in the door track
    B. dead batteries
    C. poor contact in the master door controller
    D. a main reservoir leak

12. If a car has a cracked truck frame, it is advisable to cut out the brakes on this car in order to

    A. reduce the strain on the truck frame
    B. prevent strain on the brake rigging which may be out of line
    C. prevent brake cylinder vibration which may cause further cracking
    D. prevent stuck brakes from occurring because of the cracked frame

13. When a door engine thermal cutout on an R-17 car is tripped,

    A. the affected door will operate rapidly
    B. the door will not operate
    C. air will be released from the closing cylinder
    D. it can be reset from the conductor's operating position

14. A car is reported for striking platforms. A possible cause for which a car inspector should check is

    A. improper setting of height adjusters
    B. cracked safety hanger
    C. worn bolster wear plate
    D. worn motor support

15. If the brakes drag on one car of a ten-car train, a POSSIBLE trouble could be

    A. worn brake shoes
    B. closed conductor's valve
    C. a strong brake cylinder release spring
    D. a broken brake cylinder release spring

16. If a car has a list, a POSSIBLE cause could be a

    A. cracked safety hanger
    B. broken swing link
    C. broken radius bar
    D. cracked pedestal casting wear plate

17. Small amounts of slack in the brake rigging of a car

A. must always be taken up manually
B. always indicate a broken brake rod
C. are taken care of automatically
D. never occur because a rigid brake rigging system is used

18. Safety hangers are provided on the trucks for protection of the spring plank in case of the breaking of a(n) 18.____

    A. bolster spring
    B. equalizer spring
    C. journal box
    D. swing link

19. The car part which passes through the truck center casting is the 19.____

    A. drawbar pin
    B. swing motion hanger pin
    C. straddle bar
    D. king pin

20. A POSSIBLE cause for a slow pneumatically operated door could be 20.____

    A. a defective master door controller
    B. excessive main reservoir pressure
    C. a partially clogged speed plug orifice
    D. a grounded synchronizing wire

KEY (CORRECT ANSWERS)

1.	A	11.	A
2.	B	12.	A
3.	D	13.	B
4.	D	14.	A
5.	A	15.	D
6.	C	16.	B
7.	D	17.	C
8.	D	18.	D
9.	A	19.	D
10.	D	20.	C

TEST 3

DIRECTIONS: Each question or incomplete statement is followed by several suggested answers or completions. Select the one that BEST answers the question or completes the statement. *PRINT THE LETTER OF THE CORRECT ANSWER IN THE SPACE AT THE RIGHT.*

1. When a road car inspector finds it necessary to cut out the brakes on a car, he SHOULD

    A. close both angle cocks
    B. pull the main switch
    C. open the drain cocks
    D. close the brake cutout cock

    1.____

2. If a road car inspector finds a car with abnormal cylinder piston travel, a POSSIBLE cause that he could check for would be

    A. tight brake shoe key
    B. a weak release spring
    C. a bent pull rod
    D. a slight leak in the head gasket

    2.____

3. After properly cutting out a defective door of a car in service, the road car inspector SHOULD

    A. make certain that all doors of this car are cut out
    B. properly report the defective door for further disposition
    C. mark the defective door for destruction
    D. ride this train to the terminal for observation

    3.____

4. Brake shoes that are worn to the condemning point are

    A. scrapped
    B. reclaimed by a *build-up* welding process
    C. continued in service after wear pads have been attached
    D. removed and used on work cars

    4.____

5. The truck part that must be dismantled before a pair of wheels can be removed from a truck frame is the

    A. pedestal binder   B. motor nose support
    C. transom plate   D. end frame

    5.____

6. The MOST likely cause for a stiff drawbar would be a

    A. dry carrier yoke
    B. low coupler head
    C. worn carrier wear plate
    D. drawbar pin that is too long

    6.____

7. The elliptic spring seat rests directly on the

    A. truck bolster   B. pedestal casting
    C. spring plank   D. transom

    7.____

8. A journal brass may be replaced after FIRST removing the

    8.____

59

A. transom plate B. gussett plate
C. tapered pin D. wedge keeper

9. The king pin passes through the

    A. drawbar and bolster
    B. car body center easting
    C. center plate and side frame
    D. coupler and truck center plate

10. If a road car inspector finds that the doors of one car of a ten-car train fail to open, a POSSIBLE cause that he should check for is

    A. a defective door master controller
    B. a blown fuse
    C. obstructed door tracks
    D. a door cut-out switch in open position

11. A CORRECT measurement of brake shoe clearance could be made with the brakes fully

    A. applied with a service application
    B. applied with an emergency application
    C. applied and all slack out of the brake rigging
    D. released

12. The seriousness of a wheel flat spot can BEST be determined by

    A. its color B. ridging in the spot
    C. hardness of spot D. its length

13. The truck bolster is

    A. beneath the elliptic springs
    B. under truck transoms
    C. seated on elliptic springs between transoms
    D. used to carry the elliptic springs

14. The bolster height adjuster is MAINLY used to compensate for _____ wear.

    A. wheel B. bolster
    C. spring seat D. axle

15. Of the following defects, the MOST serious is

    A. wheel flat spot B. cracked axle
    C. hot journal D. sagged elliptic spring

16. If a road car inspector finds a car has a noisy truck, a likely trouble would be

    A. worn wheels B. worn slack adjuster
    C. worn brake shoes D. broken teeth on pinion

17. The number of trip cocks on a car truck in passenger service is

    A. 3 B. 2 C. 1 D. 0

18. The car motor is supported by the

A. swing hangers and motor nose support
B. axle bearings and swing hangers
C. axle bearings and motor nose support
D. swing hangers and spring planks

19. An IMPORTANT purpose of the journal bearing keeper is to

    A. serve as an oil retainer
    B. keep dust out of the journal bearing
    C. reduce journal bearing wear
    D. limit axle end clearance

20. An IMPORTANT reason for replacing a cracked dust guard is to prevent

    A. the oil from leaking out
    B. steel particles from getting into the bearing
    C. noisy operation
    D. the dust guard from being damaged further

KEY (CORRECT ANSWERS)

1.	D	11.	D
2.	C	12.	D
3.	B	13.	C
4.	A	14.	A
5.	A	15.	B
6.	A	16.	D
7.	C	17.	C
8.	C	18.	C
9.	B	19.	D
10.	B	20.	B

TEST 4

DIRECTIONS: Each question or incomplete statement is followed by several suggested answers or completions. Select the one that BEST answers the question or completes the statement. *PRINT THE LETTER OF THE CORRECT ANSWER IN THE SPACE AT THE RIGHT.*

1. A side door panel may be removed by first disconnecting the door 1.____

    A. engine   B. track   C. lock   D. levers

2. The MAIN reason for using lubricants sparingly on a car is to 2.____

    A. save time
    B. keep costs down
    C. prevent throwing or spreading of lubricant to undesirable points
    D. prevent lubricants from drying in place

3. Penetrating oil is useful for 3.____

    A. lubricating heavy mechanical parts
    B. freeing rusted car body screws
    C. lubricating small electrical units
    D. lubricating a car body center casting

4. During a brake application, the brake shoe is lined up with the car wheel by means of a(n) 4.____

    A. wheel flange   B. equalizing bar
    C. radius bar   D. slack adjuster

5. Emergency brake staff is connected to brake system by means of 5.____

    A. gears   B. chain   C. levers   D. cable

6. Car heaters are GENERALLY cleaned by 6.____

    A. dipping in mineral spirits
    B. washing with tri-sodium phosphate
    C. blowing with compressed air
    D. scraping the heater elements

7. A car wheel tread is usually checked for wear by using a _____ gage. 7.____

    A. contour   B. depth
    C. micrometer   D. surface

8. Fire extinguishers in cars are refilled with 8.____

    A. soda ash   B. carbon tetrachloride
    C. carbon dioxide   D. special foam solution

9. Safety hangers are provided on cars for protecting the 9.____

    A. pedestal casting   B. brake hangers
    C. transom   D. spring plank

10. The MAIN purpose of an anti-climber is to 10.____

A. increase strength of car body end sill
B. prevent low flange wheels from climbing a rail on a curve
C. prevent cars from telescoping
D. increase car body stability on super-elevated track

11. If the armature of a door opening magnet valve should become stuck, then it is LIKELY that the door will

    A. become inoperative
    B. close slower
    C. open faster
    D. open slower

12. If a pneumatically operated door of a car partly opens while a train is in motion, a LIKELY trouble would be

    A. defective door lock
    B. door closing magnet is energized
    C. no air pressure is present in the main reservoir
    D. the spring pressure on the operating lever is too high

13. A road car inspector should cut out the brakes on a car if the

    A. doors on the car are defective
    B. car brake shoes are worn
    C. car has cracked truck frame
    D. safety hanger is loose

14. If there is pneumatic trouble on a door, but the electrical circuits are okay, then the

    A. door can still be operated electrically
    B. door will be inoperative
    C. motorman's indication light will fail to work properly
    D. conductor's signal light will fail to work properly

15. If a road car inspector finds a train in a station has a missing brake shoe, it would be advisable for him to

    A. readjust the slack adjuster
    B. tighten the brake shoe key
    C. check the shoe head for damage
    D. make a spot check to see whether the missing shoe is along the track near the train

16. A MOST likely cause for a car door striking the inside of its door pocket would be a

    A. loose or misaligned door track
    B. worn door engine gear rack
    C. worn shieve roller
    D. defective lock bar

17. If a road car inspector finds a shoe paddle jammed in back of a side door on a car in passenger service preventing it from opening, he SHOULD

    A. remove the obstructing paddle
    B. ask the motorman about this condition

C. remove the paddle and repair the door properly
D. assume this door is defective

18. If the distance between two car wheels on the same axle is greater than the standard wheel gage, it is LIKELY that

   A. these wheels will develop sharp flanges in service
   B. the journal bearings will wear faster
   C. no appreciable damage will be caused
   D. the car body will list

19. If the cylinder head gasket on the small cylinder of a pneumatic differential door engine is leaking, it would PROBABLY result in the door

   A. closing more slowly
   B. opening more slowly
   C. opening more rapidly
   D. not operating at all

20. If upon inspection of a journal box babbitt chips are observed in the waste packing, it would MOST likely indicate that

   A. the waste was saturated with oil
   B. the waste was properly packed
   C. there was no tin in the babbitt
   D. journal brass had run hot

KEY (CORRECT ANSWERS)

1.	D	11.	A
2.	C	12.	A
3.	B	13.	C
4.	A	14.	B
5.	B	15.	D
6.	C	16.	A
7.	A	17.	D
8.	B	18.	A
9.	D	19.	B
10.	C	20.	D

EXAMINATION SECTION
TEST 1

DIRECTIONS: Each question or incomplete statement is followed by several suggested answers or completions. Select the one that BEST answers the question or completes the statement. *PRINT THE LETTER OF THE CORRECT ANSWER IN THE SPACE AT THE RIGHT.*

Questions 1-6.

DIRECTIONS: Questions 1 through 6, inclusive, are to be answered on the basis of the following paragraphs which trace the air flow in *SMEE* airbrake equipment for the condition where the motorman's Brake Valve is in the *Handle Off* position. Certain key words have been omitted in this description, and in each resulting blank space, you will find instead an identifying number. For each question, you are to select the CORRECT wording corresponding to each of the identifying numbers.

TRACING OF THE AIR IN SMEE AIR BRAKE EQUIPMENT WITH THE BRAKE VALVE IN *HANDLE OFF* POSITION

As the compressor operates, air is drawn from the atmosphere through a strainer into the compressor cylinders, then through a cooling coil into the No. 1 Main Reservoir; thence, through a rubber hose and cooling coils into the No. 2 Main Reservoir and through a metal pipe, cut-out cock, and J-Filter into the M-3-A Feed Valve. On the R-22 cars, air passing through the Feed Valve is reduced from Main Reservoir Pressure of 135-150 psi to __(1)__ pressure.

Feed Valve Pressure Air then flows into the Supply Pipe with branches to the Vent Valve, Reset Magnet Valve, Application Magnet Valve, Whistle Valve, Uncoupling Valve, A-1 Supply Unit, and ME-42 Brake Valve. From another branch in the Supply Line, Feed Valve Air flows past a ball check and branches into three directions:
    Branch (a) to the __(2)__ Valve;
    Branch (b) through a __(3)__ Valve into the Supply
      Reservoir;
    Branch (c) to the Charging Valve.
Feed Valve Air from the Charging Valve flows to the Quick Action Chamber and to the left-hand side of the Vent Valve Emergency Piston, forcing the piston to its __(4)__ position.

Feed Valve Air then is connected to the lower side of the Double Check Valve, forcing it to the right, connecting Feed Valve Air to the Bypass and Ball Check Valves of the __(5)__ Valve.

The air at the Bypass Valve lifts the check and flows to the Relay Valve, which closes the Brake Cylinder exhaust and opens the __(6)__ Valve connecting the Supply Reservoir Air to the Brake Cylinders, forcing the piston out, thus applying the brake shoes to the car wheels.

1. Of the following, the MOST appropriate pressure to insert in the blank space identified by (1) is

    A. atmospheric
    B. 70 psi
    C. 110 psi
    D. 150 psi

2. The valve which BEST describes (2) is

    A. Safety
    B. Drain
    C. B-Relay
    D. Unloader

3. The valve which BEST describes (3) is _____ cock.

    A. cut-out
    B. drain-
    C. trip-
    D. load-

4. The position which BEST describes (4) is

    A. Emergency
    B. Release
    C. Running
    D. Service

5. The valve which BEST describes (5) is

    A. Conductor's
    B. Whistle
    C. Unloader
    D. Variable-load

6. The valve which BEST describes (6) is

    A. Inshot
    B. Application
    C. Safety
    D. Vent

7. Four air reservoir tanks shown in the sketch to the right have been filled with air by the air compressor. If the main line air gage reads 160 psi, then the tank air gage will read _____ psi.

    A. 0
    B. 25
    C. 50
    D. 160

8. If all valves are closed in the air tank shown in the accompanying sketch, which valves must be opened to move the pistons to the right?
   A. 1 and 2
   B. 2 and 3
   C. 1, 3, and 4
   D. 2, 3, and 4

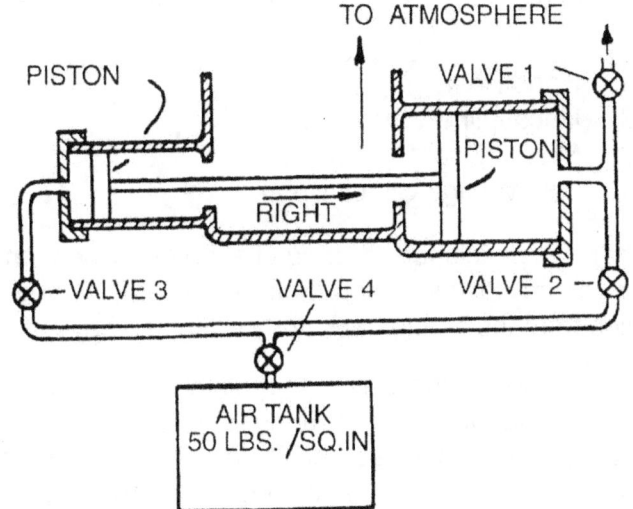

9. Each of the four procedures given below describes a possible way for putting together the various parts shown in the sketch of the assembly at the right. The PROPER procedure is:
   A. 1 thru 3 and into 2; 6 over 5; and 4 on 1
   B. 4 onto 1; 1 thru 3; 2 and 6 on 1; and 5 thru 3 and 6
   C. 5 thru 3; 1 thru 3; and into 6; 6 over 5; and 4 and 2 onto 1
   D. 4 onto 1; 1 into 6; 5 thru 3 and 6; and 1 thru 3 and into 2

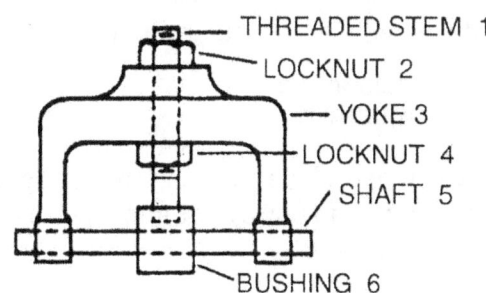

10. In the sketch at the right, there are five lamp sockets, one of which is empty. Under these conditions, the voltage E is MOST NEARLY _____ volts.
    A. 0
    B. 240
    C. 360
    D. 600

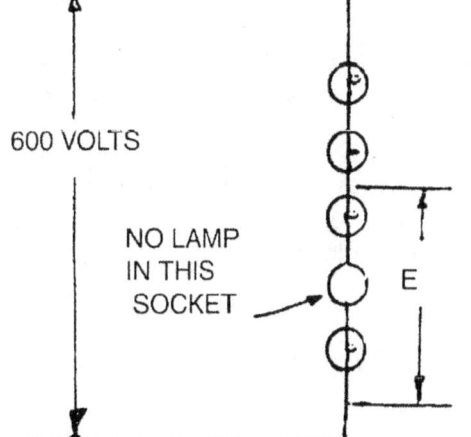

11. Commutators are found on
    A. traction motors
    B. brake cylinders
    C. master controllers
    D. brake valves

12. Which one of the following units is located in the number 2 cab of an R-40 type subway car?   12._____

    A. Hand Brake
    B. Uncoupling Valve
    C. Master Door Controller
    D. Low Voltage Circuit Breaker 1

13. A car has developed a serious flat on one wheel and has been placed temporarily on a lay-up track for inspection. Before this car is moved to the repair shop, which is about five miles from the lay-up track, the car should have   13._____

    A. the wheel removed and replaced with a good wheel
    B. the flat built up with weld metal
    C. the truck removed and replaced with an overhauled truck
    D. nothing done to it and should be moved *as is.*

14. The device generally used by the motorman to indicate that he needs assistance from the Road Car Inspector on the station platform is the   14._____

    A. telephone   B. whistle
    C. buzzer   D. headlights

15. Which one of the following relays regulates both the rate of acceleration and the dynamic braking of a subway car traction motor?   15._____
    _____ Relay.

    A. Reset   B. Current Limit
    C. Line Switch   D. Emergency

16. Descending from the R-44 train to the roadway can be done safely only from the _____ end of a(n) _____ car.   16._____

    A. #1; *A*   B. #2; *B*   C. #2; *A*   D. #3; *B*

17. If an RCI is working around a train when a train crew is not present, an IMPORTANT safety precaution he should take is to   17._____

    A. lock the storm doors at both ends of the train
    B. disconnect couplers at both ends of the train
    C. connect third rail jumpers at both ends of the train
    D. place a red flag in front of the lead car

18. Which one of the following conditions would present the GREATEST danger for passengers on a train?   18._____
    A

    A. hot journal box   B. cracked axle
    C. flat wheel   D. sagged elliptical spring

19. The circuit shown in the sketch at the right is known as a _____ circuit.
    A. full wave bridge rectifier
    B. multivibrator
    C. uni-junction transistor timing
    D. audio amplifier

19.____

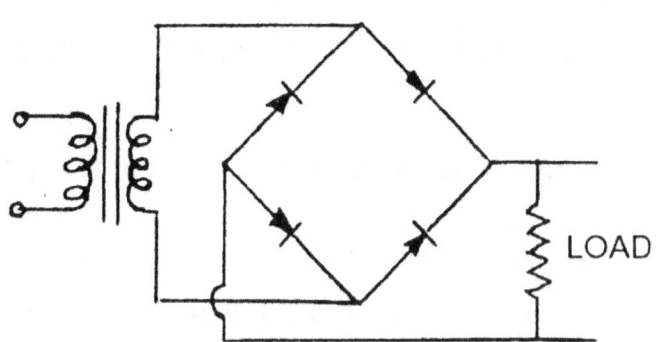

20. What should be the condition of the brake equipment before a motorman starts to move a passenger train?

20.____

   A. Air brakes should be cut out on all cars.
   B. Hand brakes should be set up on all cars.
   C. Main reservoir line and brake pipe angle cocks should be open on all cars.
   D. Brake pipes should be open between cars.

21. What is the TOTAL power taken by a D.C. device drawing one milliampere of current at one kilovolt?
    One

21.____

   A. milliwatt   B. watt
   C. kilowatt   D. megawatt

22. What is the MOST important function of the relay as used in the circuit shown in the sketch at the right? To
    A. reverse polarity on the lamps
    B. limit line voltage to the lamps
    C. measure an overload on the lamp circuit
    D. control the high 600 volt circuit by the low 32 volt circuit

22.____

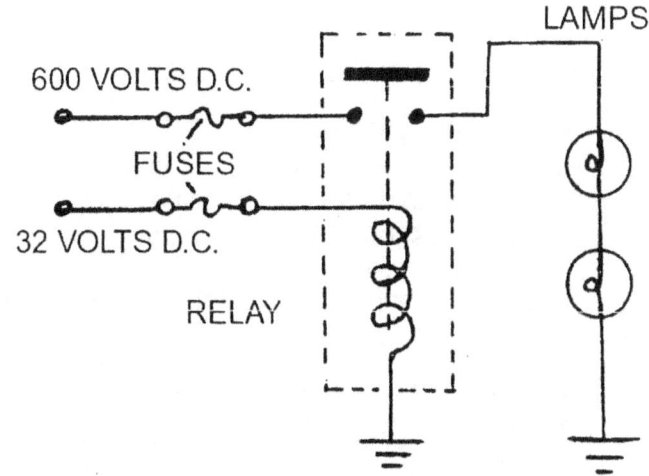

23. In the sketch at the right, the male key which should fit the slotted cylinder is
    A. A
    B. B
    C. C
    D. D

23.____

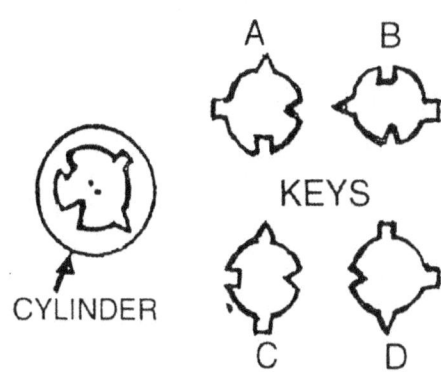

24. The function of a step-down transformer is to decrease the

   A. current   B. voltage   C. power   D. frequency

25. Thermal relays are used in motor circuits to protect against

   A. underspeed   B. underload
   C. overspeed   D. overload

26. The connections for a D.C. voltmeter are observed to move backwards when they are applied to two test points of a circuit.
   This means that the

   A. meter is defective
   B. electrical contact is poor at the test points
   C. meter leads are reversed
   D. second test point is part of an A.C. circuit

27. One indication that a car wheel has been severely overheated is that the

   A. wheel has turned blue
   B. motor will no longer take power
   C. brakes can no longer be applied
   D. car has lost brake pipe pressure

28. The third rail emergency jumpers are for use in an emergency to carry current to motors, when a train is on a gap, or when snow and ice prevent the contact shoes from making contact with the third rail.
   The SAFEST procedure to follow in using the jumper is FIRST to apply the spike of the jumper to the and then apply the opposite end of the jumper to the

   A. third rail; shoe of the car
   B. contact shoe of the car; third rail
   C. contact shoe of the car; contact shoe of the same truck on the other side of the car
   D. contact shoe of the car; ground

29. The S-16-C Compressor Governor in the SMEE brake equipment is designed to automatically

   A. operate the brake cylinder in an emergency condition
   B. cut in electro-dynamic braking at speeds higher than 15 miles per hour
   C. control the compressor air pressure between minimum and maximum values
   D. prevent the pressure in the supply reservoir from becoming larger than the pressure in the No. 1 main reservoir

30. Rule 54 of the Transit Authority describes flagging and signaling as it applies to moving trains.
    One section of this rule states that moving the hand, a flag, a light, or any other object to and fro across the track means

    A. proceed at normal full speed
    B. stop
    C. stop and then proceed at slow speed
    D. reduce speed to one-half normal speed

31. The Ohio Brass Form 70 coupler on the R-44 cars is inspected for distortion and wear by using

    A. two dial gages and one caliper micrometer
    B. two dial gages, one caliper micrometer, and one depth micrometer
    C. a hook gage, a coupler face gage, and two buffing-pulling face gages
    D. two telescopic gages, one depth micrometer, and one caliper micrometer

32. The electric portion of the coupler on the R-44 car has both fixed contact pins and retracting contact pins.
    In the extended position, the advance of those pins beyond the coupler face is gaged with a

    A. feeler gage
    B. depth micrometer
    C. telescopic gage
    D. Go and No-Go gage, T-307

33. On married-pair type car equipment, the motor generator is provided on

    A. only the odd-numbered cars
    B. both cars of a pair
    C. either the odd-numbered or the even-numbered car of a pair
    D. only the even-numbered cars

34. Of the following types of fire extinguishers, the one that should be used to extinguish an electrical fire is the _____ type.

    A. carbon-tetrachloride
    B. foam
    C. carbon dioxide
    D. soda-acid

35. On an R-22 subway car, it is observed that the same end of each fluorescent tube is dim. The PROBABLE cause of this is

    A. an under-voltage condition
    B. an automatic timer failure
    C. an over-voltage condition
    D. failure of the momentary switch

36. The motors on the door operators for the R-40 cars are operated with _____ volts _____.

    A. 18; D.C.   B. 32; D.C.   C. 115; A.C.   D. 600; D.C.

37. A road car inspector notes that the motorman's indication is flickering. 37.____
Of the following, the MOST probable cause of this condition is

    A. high air pressure   B. low air pressure
    C. a blown fuse   D. an intermittent s

38. In the report of an accident, the information which is MOST likely to be useful in decreas- 38.____
ing the recurrence of similar accidents is the

    A. type of medical assistance obtained
    B. cause of the accident
    C. name of the foreman
    D. number of people involved

39. If train speeds on a particular track are to be temporarily reduced to NO more than 10 39.____
miles per hour without the stationing of a flagman, the number of yellow lamps that
should be placed on the track is

    A. 1   B. 2   C. 3   D. 4

40. On the R-44 cars, the end door unlock lights will illuminate when 40.____

    A. the blue light appears on the motorman's console
    B. the red light appears on the side of the car
    C. either the cab door or the end door is unlocked
    D. both the cab door and the end door are open

KEY (CORRECT ANSWERS)

1.	C	11.	A	21.	B	31.	C
2.	C	12.	C	22.	D	32.	D
3.	A	13.	B	23.	A	33.	D
4.	A	14.	B	24.	B	34.	C
5.	D	15.	B	25.	D	35.	B
6.	B	16.	A	26.	C	36.	B
7.	D	17.	D	27.	A	37.	D
8.	C	18.	B	28.	B	38.	B
9.	B	19.	A	29.	C	39.	C
10.	D	20.	C	30.	B	40.	C

TEST 2

DIRECTIONS: Each question or incomplete statement is followed by several suggested answers or completions. Select the one that BEST answers the question or completes the statement. *PRINT THE LETTER OF THE CORRECT ANSWER IN THE SPACE AT THE RIGHT.*

1. Of the following reasons for which a road car inspector should be familiar with first aid methods, the MAIN one is that   1.____

    A. the Transit Authority may avoid a lawsuit if the injury is taken care of promptly
    B. prompt attention to the injured will avoid train delays
    C. he will be prepared to act quickly in an emergency
    D. this will reduce the need for an ambulance in case of an accident

2. While waiting for the ambulance to take away a passenger who has fallen on the station platform and broken his leg, the road car inspector should   2.____

    A. get the emergency stretcher and place the passenger on it
    B. secure a third rail slipper and use it as a splint on the leg
    C. move the passenger to a spot where he will be out of the way of traffic
    D. make the passenger as comfortable as possible without moving him

3. The MAIN purpose of the periodic inspection of transit facilities and equipment is to   3.____

    A. keep the maintainers busy during slack periods
    B. enable the maintainers to become more familiar with these facilities and equipment
    C. uncover minor faults before they become serious
    D. encourage better care of Transit Authority property

4. When an unusual situation arises and it would take too long to contact your foreman for advice, the BEST procedure for you as a road car inspector to follow is to   4.____

    A. take no action since it might be the wrong one
    B. confer with the motorman on the best action to take
    C. confer with the conductor on the best action to take
    D. act according to your best judgment

5. A road car inspector is not permitted to give a passenger a description of any lost article which has been found because   5.____

    A. he may give an incorrect description
    B. this might aid the passenger to make a false claim
    C. the rules forbid employees from talking to passengers
    D. this might interfere with the inspector's work

6. Of the following electrical circuits, the MAIN one that a road car inspector should have a working knowledge is the   6.____

    A. signal circuits   B. power distribution circuits
    C. negative return circuits   D. car circuits

7. Wooden wedges are sometimes applied to the trip cocks of certain subway cars MAINLY to prevent undesired tripping by

    A. ballast
    B. vibration
    C. snow
    D. track debris

8. When a train is being removed from service, the road car inspector should assist the train crew in

    A. discharging the passengers
    B. cutting out the side doors
    C. locking the storm doors
    D. closing all windows

9. Of the following train defects on one of the middle cars of a train, the one for which it would be LEAST necessary for a road car inspector to ride the train to the terminal is

    A. a hot journal
    B. a grounded shoe beam
    C. cut out brakes
    D. tied-up broken brake rigging

10. If all the doors on one side of an R-22 car fail to open, the MOST likely cause is a

    A. blown No. 24 fuse
    B. blown DC1 fuse
    C. blown LI fuse
    D. door engine circuit breaker

11. When a road car inspector finds it necessary to open the main knife switch of a subway car, he must make sure that

    A. the electric portions are retrieved
    B. all 600-volt panel board switches are open
    C. the compressor is running
    D. all 600-volt panel board switches are closed

12. When a road car inspector finds it necessary to cut out the brakes on a car, he should

    A. pull the main switch
    B. close both angle cocks
    C. close the brake cut-out cock
    D. open the drain cocks

13. If a guard light remains lit after the conductor has closed all the doors on a train, the road car inspector should know that this condition would

    A. require replacement of the guard light bulb
    B. mean loss of indication to both motorman and conductor
    C. affect only the conductor's indication
    D. affect only the motorman's indication

14. A road car inspector when down on the tracks in the vicinity of track switches should be extra careful in following safety precautions since the ties

    A. have very narrow spacing
    B. may be slippery from grease accumulation
    C. have very large spacing
    D. are likely to be badly split

15. Cars are equipped with a by-pass button located at the motorman's indication box. The MAIN purpose of this button is to permit the by-passing of the

    A. door relay
    B. master controller
    C. reverser
    D. pilot valve

16. On a subway car, the battery voltage is used for

    A. heaters
    B. compressor motors
    C. traction motors
    D. door control circuits

17. On an 11-car R-36 train set up for one-man conductor operation, the number of drum switches that must be in the THRU position is

    A. 9 B. 11 C. 18 D. 22

18. The pinion and gear on the propulsion motor of a car has seized and, as a result, the motor will not turn. The car has been placed on a siding. Attempts were made to free the pinion and gear but they were unsuccessful. Before this car is moved to the repair shop, the car should have

    A. the motor removed
    B. the pinion burned off
    C. all brake shoes removed
    D. the brake harness disconnected

19. Flat spots on car wheels are MOST likely to occur when the

    A. service brakes are applied
    B. train is brought to a service stop from a high speed
    C. emergency cord is pulled to stop the train
    D. train goes around a sharp curve at low speed

20. The black needle of the duplex air gage used with SMEE type brakes indicates _____ pressure.

    A. straight air
    B. brake pipe
    C. equalizing reservoir
    D. main reservoir

21. A car is equipped with the SMEE brake equipment.
    If a road car inspector is unable to close an open trip cock on the car because of a broken trip arm, he should treat this condition in the same manner as a(n)

    A. brake pipe rupture
    B. stuck hand brake
    C. overcharged feed valve
    D. compressor which is not operating

22. The rules of the Transit Authority state that employees should not make any statements concerning transit accidents except to appropriate officials of the Transit Authority.
The MOST likely reason for this rule is to

A. avoid lawsuits based on employees' statements
B. avoid conflicting testimony of employees
C. conceal facts which may be damaging to the Transit Authority
D. avoid the possibility of unofficial statements being taken and used as official statements

23. Employees of the Car Maintenance Department are required to report defective equipment to their superiors even if the maintenance of such equipment is the responsibility of another department.
The MAIN purpose of this rule is to

A. keep the employees alert
B. reward those who keep their eyes open
C. check up on who is not doing his job
D. have repairs made before serious trouble occurs

24. The rules of the Transit Authority require that the transit police be notified first whenever an ambulance is needed.
The MOST logical reason for this rule is to

A. prevent duplication of calls
B. insure prompt response
C. permit the police to check on the need for the ambulance
D. allow time for a policeman to get to the scene of the accident

25. A road car inspector should use a *tape gauge* to measure

A. journal bearings
B. gears on traction motors
C. brake slack adjusters
D. car wheels

26. The BASIC operating principle of the dynamic braking system is that

A. the motors are reversible
B. magnetic solenoids slow down the axles
C. air operates the disc-type brakes
D. the motors operate as generators

27. A road car inspector has the authority to

A. tie down a track tripper
B. key a train by a red signal
C. remove a train from passenger service
D. operate a train on yard tracks

28. If a train is stopped at a station, a road car inspector is forbidden to

A. replace a car lighting fuse
B. replace a brake fuse
C. work on a trip cock
D. work on the circuits of the doors opposite those on the platform side

29. A road car inspector should remove power from the third rail if a train has

   A. any coupling trouble
   B. any brake trouble
   C. overcharging batteries
   D. a grounded shoe beam

30. Of the following train defects, the one MOST likely to cause locked car wheels is

   A. a worn center bearing
   B. excessive voltage
   C. a defective coupler
   D. defective traction gears

31. A road car inspector should pull the emergency alarm box to

   A. call the fire department
   B. call the transit police
   C. remove third rail power
   D. restore third rail power

32. The Transit Authority stations road car inspectors along the road MAINLY to

   A. alert Central Control in case of a train stoppage
   B. get them out of sight of the riding public
   C. minimize train delays
   D. discourage abuse of equipment by the operating forces

33. The MAIN function of a check valve in a multiple-unit car air brake system is to

   A. serve as a reducing valve
   B. permit the insertion of a check gage
   C. allow for drainage of the system
   D. permit air to flow in one direction only

34. A set of gears connects the main motor armature shaft to the car axle in order to permit the wheels to rotate at

   A. uniform speed
   B. lower speed than the armature
   C. the same speed as the armature
   D. greater speed than the armature

35. A blue light along the right-of-way between stations GENERALLY indicates the location of a(n)

   A. telephone
   B. tower
   C. crossover
   D. emergency exit

Questions 36-40.

DIRECTIONS: Questions 36 through 40 are to be answered on the basis of the standard electrical symbol shown on the following page at the right. Each symbol is identified by a number, and this number is to be used in answering these questions.

36. A *transistor* is shown at number
    A. 2
    B. 4
    C. 7
    D. 11

37. A *fuse* is shown at number
    A. 1
    B. 2
    C. 3
    D. 13

38. A *transformer* is shown at number
    A. 4
    B. 6
    C. 8
    D. 14

39. A *diode* is shown at number
    A. 1
    B. 4
    C. 11
    D. 13

40. A *ground* is shown at number
    A. 2
    B. 9
    C. 11
    D. 14

36.____
37.____
38.____
39.____
40.____

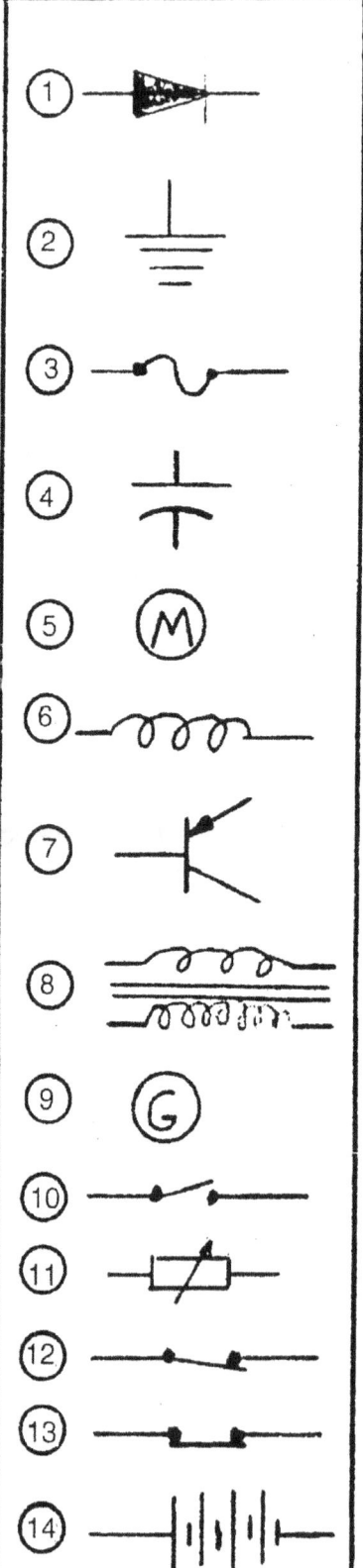

KEY (CORRECT ANSWERS)

1. C	11. B	21. A	31. C
2. D	12. C	22. D	32. C
3. C	13. B	23. D	33. D
4. D	14. B	24. A	34. B
5. B	15. A	25. D	35. A
6. D	16. D	26. D	36. C
7. C	17. C	27. C	37. C
8. A	18. B	28. D	38. C
9. C	19. C	29. D	39. A
10. B	20. B	30. D	40. A

EXAMINATION SECTION
TEST 1

DIRECTIONS: Each question or incomplete statement is followed by several suggested answers or completions. Select the one that BEST answers the question or completes the statement. *PRINT THE LETTER OF THE CORRECT ANSWER IN THE SPACE AT THE RIGHT.*

1. Of the following procedures by which a foreman may train his assistant to take his place during his absence, the one most generally acceptable as the BEST is for the foreman to

   A. guide the assistant in actually carrying out all the important procedures involved in the work he will have to do
   B. have the assistant attend group meetings and ask questions
   C. explain carefully to the assistant all the procedures involved, having him practice these procedures in the actual situation when the foreman is away
   D. put the assistant in charge of the unit for a few days to let him learn by actual practice

1.____

2. Assume that you are a foreman and you assign one of your hardest working men to do some paper work which he has never done before. Because of his inexperience, he makes many errors.
Of the following, the MOST advisable course of action for you to take is to

   A. express your appreciation for his willingness and show him how to do the work better
   B. praise his effort but reprimand him for his performance
   C. praise his work to show appreciation of his efforts
   D. say nothing but do not assign him to that work again

2.____

3. Assume that you are a foreman and a man under your supervision, who is very efficient, is constantly complaining about the type of work assigned to him. You have noticed that his complaints have a bad effect on the other men. Of the following, the BEST course of action for you to take in this situation is to

   A. ask the men to try to overlook his faults
   B. determine the cause of his attitude and try to make an adjustment in his work assignment
   C. secure his transfer to another shop or unit being supervised by a different foreman
   D. let the man make his own work assignments

3.____

4. As a foreman, you observe that one of the men under your supervision seems to be rejected by the other men of the unit and tends to stay by himself.
Of the following, the MOST advisable course of action for you to take is to

   A. ignore the situation unless it interferes with the work of the unit
   B. determine the reason and, if possible, attempt to rectify the situation
   C. have the man transferred
   D. inform the other men that they should change their attitude

4.____

5. The orders of a foreman are LEAST likely to be carried out properly if he

   A. gives detailed orders
   B. writes out his orders
   C. lacks patience when giving them
   D. asks for his orders to be repeated

6. In acquainting a new man with his duties, it would be IMPROPER for a foreman to talk about the

   A. shortcomings of the men in the gang
   B. proper method of making inspection reports
   C. rules and regulations of the department
   D. special safety precautions

7. Assume that your supervisor has issued orders for a change in work procedures that your men disagree with.
   As a foreman, it would be BEST for you to tell your men that

   A. nothing can be done about it at this time, even if their complaints are justified
   B. they should complain to the supervisor, not to you
   C. you did not like the changes yourself and tried to talk the supervisor out of them
   D. you will take up their complaints with the supervisor

8. Before turning in a report of an investigation you have made, you discover some additional information you did not know about when writing the report.
   Whether or not you rewrite your report to include this additional information should depend MAINLY on the

   A. length of the report
   B. established policy covering the subject matter of the report
   C. bearing this new information will have on the conclusions of the report
   D. number of people who will eventually review the report

9. Your assistant supervisor notifies you that several of your men have complained to him about your harsh supervisory methods.
   You should

   A. promise to ease up on the men
   B. ask him if it is fair for him to permit these men to go over your head
   C. tell him that production is always the main consideration
   D. ask him what specific acts have been considered harsh

10. If a foreman is assigned to assemble information on a certain power distribution problem, he MUST be especially careful to

    A. be impartial in collecting and presenting the information
    B. secure his information only from those in supervisory positions
    C. present the information in such a manner as to substantiate his superior's ideas on the subject
    D. discard information which seems inconsistent with previous information relating to this problem

11. The GREATEST benefit the foreman will derive from keeping complete and accurate records of his section's operations is that

    A. he will need less manpower
    B. less equipment will be needed
    C. it will be easier for him to run his section efficiently
    D. the section will run smoothly when he is out

12. One of your maintainers often slows down the work of the gang by playing practical jokes.
    The BEST way to handle this situation is to

    A. arrange for his assignment to more than his share of unpleasant jobs
    B. warn him that he must stop this practice at once
    C. ignore this situation for he will soon tire of it
    D. ask your superior to transfer him to another gang

13. In setting up a work schedule for a special job, it is LEAST important for you to know

    A. the pay rate of the various men assigned to you
    B. when the employees will be available
    C. the approximate time required to complete the job
    D. when the material for the job will be available

14. The BEST way to handle a helper's grievance against a fellow worker which you know has little merit is to

    A. acknowledge the complaint but take no action
    B. start it through the standard grievance procedure
    C. warn the man that complaints of this sort make him subject to ridicule
    D. discuss the grievance with the helper pointing out its weakness

15. A foreman would be personally to blame for inefficiency resulting from

    A. improper planning of work assignments
    B. unforeseen delays in delivery of material
    C. departmental policy of job rotation
    D. frequent labor turnover

16. Foremen are required to submit written reports of all unusual occurrences promptly.
    The BEST reason for such promptness is that

    A. there is always a tendency to do a better job under pressure
    B. the employee will not be as likely to forget to make the report
    C. the report will tend to be more accurate as to facts
    D. the report may be too long if made at an employee's convenience

17. A good way of obtaining high quality work from his men is for the foreman to

    A. give the men unusual privileges
    B. compliment the men after each job
    C. maintain a vigorous interest in each job
    D. individually assist the men on each job

18. Suggestions on improving methods of doing work, when submitted by a new employee, should be

    A. disregarded because he is too unfamiliar with the work to be able to submit any worthwhile ideas
    B. examined for possible merit because the new men may have a fresh viewpoint
    C. ignored because it would only make the old employees resentful
    D. examined only for the purpose of judging the new man

19. The MOST convincing reason for the setting of a time limit on a particular job by the foreman would be that

    A. maximum production can only be achieved in this way
    B. this particular job is urgent
    C. the men will thus be kept continuously busy
    D. the best quality of work is achieved in this manner

20. A foreman finds that he very frequently has to take disciplinary action against various members of his gang. He should

    A. realize that he has a group of troublemakers on his hands
    B. ask the union delegate to take action
    C. ask to be transferred to a less troublesome gang
    D. analyze his own supervisory methods

21. You receive a special assignment from your foreman calling for the use of equipment which you do not think is suitable for the job.
    You should

    A. immediately call this to his attention
    B. carry out your instructions as received
    C. substitute the equipment you believe to be most suitable
    D. consult with your gang on what to do

22. Of the following, the situation which would MOST severely test a foreman's supervisory skill would be the

    A. assignment of a regular job which must be expedited
    B. absorption into the group under his supervision of a number of men newly transferred to the bus shops
    C. assignment to replace a foreman who has retired
    D. attempt to improve good housekeeping on the job

23. It would be POOR practice for a foreman to

    A. personally instruct a maintainer in a difficult maintenance procedure
    B. learn the relative abilities of his men by observing the quality of their work
    C. explain to his immediate supervisor why work output decreased during a certain week
    D. complain about the quality of a maintainer's work to the man's co-workers

24. If, after careful thought, you have definitely decided that one of your men should be disciplined, it is MOST important for you to realize that
    A. discipline is the best tool for leading men
    B. discipline should be severe in order to get the best results
    C. the discipline should be delayed so that its full force can be felt
    D. the man should know why he is being disciplined

25. It is important for a supervisor to take prompt action upon requests from subordinates MAINLY because
    A. delays in making decisions mean that they must then be made on the basis of facts which can no longer be up-to-date
    B. favorable action on such requests is more likely to result when a decision is made quickly
    C. it is an indication that the supervisor has his work well organized
    D. promptness in such matters helps maintain good employee morale

KEY (CORRECT ANSWERS)

1. A		11. C	
2. A		12. B	
3. B		13. A	
4. B		14. D	
5. C		15. A	
6. A		16. C	
7. D		17. C	
8. C		18. B	
9. D		19. B	
10. A		20. D	

21. A
22. B
23. D
24. D
25. D

TEST 2

DIRECTIONS: Each question or incomplete statement is followed by several suggested answers or completions. Select the one that BEST answers the question or completes the statement. *PRINT THE LETTER OF THE CORRECT ANSWER IN THE SPACE AT THE RIGHT.*

1. A foreman opens a first aid kit and gives a band-aid to one of his helpers. After using the kit, the foreman should

    A. return the kit to the medical department and obtain a sealed kit
    B. replace the band-aid with one from any kit not presently being used
    C. inform the medical department, replace the band-aid, and use the kit again
    D. use the kit again *as is* and add the band-aid to the kit's list of missing materials

2. A foreman should know when to refer a matter to his assistant supervisor and when to handle it himself.
Of the following, the situation which a foreman would be MOST correct in referring to his assistant supervisor for handling is one where

    A. a maintainer has made a poor cable splice
    B. there is a breakdown of recently purchased power tools
    C. some of the foreman's men habitually return late from lunch
    D. there is a disagreement between one of the foreman's helpers and one of his maintainers

3. A foreman is required to make routine checks on each of his maintainers. The manner in which these checks should be made is AT LEAST daily by

    A. telephone and daily by personal contact
    B. telephone and weekly through personal contact
    C. personal contact and by telephone as warranted
    D. telephone and bi-weekly through personal contact

4. A foreman should NOT accept a grievance presented to him by a maintainer _____ after the event he is complaining about has taken place.

    A. orally one day
    B. in writing two days
    C. orally four days
    D. in writing seven days

5. A foreman to whom a maintainer presents a grievance should communicate his decision to the maintainer, after receiving the grievance, within

    A. 24 hours   B. 48 hours   C. 5 days   D. 7 days

6. As a foreman, it is necessary for you to know that your men are learning the work properly.
A good practical method for a construction foreman to use in determining this in the case of a new helper is to

    A. assume that if he asks no questions, he knows the work
    B. ask the other men how this man is making out
    C. follow-up and inspect the work which is assigned to him
    D. question him directly on construction methods

7. Suppose the various jobs under your supervision are frequently delayed because the men await your arrival to make decisions before proceeding with the work.
As a foreman, the MOST helpful conclusion for you to draw from this is that

   A. the jobs given to you are generally more difficult than the average
   B. your orders and instructions may not have been sufficiently clear or complete
   C. you have incurred the men's dislike and should look for the cause
   D. the men under your supervision lack initiative and need encouragement

8. It would be POOR supervision on a foreman's part if he

   A. consulted his assistant supervisor on unusual problems
   B. asked an experienced maintainer for his opinion on the method of doing a special installation job
   C. allowed a cooling-off period of several days before giving one of his men a deserved reprimand
   D. made it a policy to avoid criticizing a man in front of his co-workers

9. Many management experts believe that it is advantageous for a foreman to learn (without asking directly) as much as possible about his men, even personal matters about their families.
The LOGICAL advantage to the foreman of taking such personal interest in the men is that he will

   A. know how to assign jobs so as to get them done with the least friction
   B. know when excuses for absence are valid
   C. be able to advise the men when they bring in their home problems
   D. establish friendships which are likely to improve employee morale

10. As a foreman, it is advisable for you to keep records of your jobs for future reference. Assume that in reviewing your records you find that whenever a certain maintainer has been one of the men assigned to a job, the job has taken appreciably longer than other similar jobs. In this case, you would do BEST to

    A. consult your assistant supervisor on the appropriate disciplinary action to be taken
    B. give closer supervision to future jobs to which this man is assigned
    C. take this fact into consideration when making up service rating reports
    D. warn the man against deliberate slowness so that he knows that you are aware of the situation

11. Of the following, the quality which contributes MOST toward good foremanship is the ability to

    A. be considered as *one of the boys*
    B. keep from worrying
    C. get work out
    D. be forceful

12. If a foreman establishes a social relationship with his men, the result is MOST likely to be

    A. loss of discipline
    B. fewer accidents
    C. increased respect from the men
    D. greatly increased work output

13. If a foreman has a maintainer working for him who is lacking in self-confidence, but is otherwise capable, the foreman should

    A. give the man a forceful pep talk
    B. criticize his work severely to hurt his pride
    C. find out if the condition is caused by home problems
    D. compliment the man's work whenever possible

14. Before attempting to settle a group grievance as compared to an individual case, the foreman should

    A. check the record of previous complaints of each man in the group
    B. clear his decision with the assistant supervisor
    C. check with each man to be sure his decision will be satisfactory
    D. defer decision as long as possible to give the group a chance to forget the grievance

15. In assigning a job which may have an unusual hazard, it is BEST to

    A. give the assignment to a senior member of your gang
    B. reward the employee assigned
    C. assign it to an employee requiring disciplinary action
    D. ask for volunteers before making the assignment

16. A newly appointed helper has made a blunder which resulted in injury to a maintainer. As a foreman, you should certainly

    A. recommend dismissal of the new helper
    B. ignore the incident unless it recurs
    C. study the accident for remedial action
    D. reprimand the maintainer for not properly instructing the helper

17. You notice a maintainer doing a job in a manner that you believe is unsafe. He tells you that he is doing it the way his previous foreman taught him.
    Of the following, the BEST action for you to take is to

    A. show the maintainer how you want it done
    B. let him continue and see if it turns out all right
    C. reassign the job to someone you know will do it your way
    D. speak to the other foreman to see if the maintainer told you the truth

18. The MOST dependable standard by which a foreman can judge the quality of a particular repair job done by his men is   18._____

    A. the number of man-hours it took to do the job
    B. how well the completed job holds up in service
    C. the way his men react to his supervision of the job
    D. how closely his instructions were followed by the men who did the job

19. As a foreman, one of the BEST ways of cooperating with your superior would be to   19._____

    A. constantly bring him new ideas for him to determine the advantages and disadvantages
    B. ask him to decide all problems which may arise
    C. accept full responsibility for the work assigned to your men
    D. constantly bring him all the details of the work

20. Subordinates are BEST encouraged in improving deficient work by   20._____

    A. criticism
    B. punishment
    C. patient demonstration of proper metods
    D. withholding of benefits

KEY (CORRECT ANSWERS)

1.	A	11.	C
2.	B	12.	A
3.	B	13.	D
4.	D	14.	B
5.	B	15.	D
6.	C	16.	C
7.	B	17.	A
8.	C	18.	B
9.	A	19.	C
10.	B	20.	C

TEST 3

DIRECTIONS: Each question or incomplete statement is followed by several suggested answers or completions. Select the one that BEST answers the question or completes the statement. *PRINT THE LETTER OF THE CORRECT ANSWER IN THE SPACE AT THE RIGHT.*

1. Assume you are called to another location before this job is complete. Your PROPER supervisory action before leaving for the other location is to

    A. call the men together and assign each one enough work to cover the period of your absence
    B. clearly designate an experienced maintainer to be in charge during your absence
    C. report your intended movement to the supervisor and request instructions
    D. place a set of written instructions in the new booth and inform each man of your action

2. A helper whom you do not know is promoted to fill a maintainer vacancy in your section, while a man you believe to be very good and whom you would like to have seen promoted remains a helper in your section because his name is two places further down on the civil service promotion list.
   In this case, your BEST procedure as foreman would be to

    A. convince the new man that he should transfer to another section as soon as a vacancy occurs
    B. have the helper you like transferred to another section to avoid friction
    C. ask your supervisor for additional jobs so as to be able to increase your quota of maintainers
    D. fit the new man into your section as quickly as possible

3. If a foreman assigns an assistant foreman to supervise a group of emergency laborers temporarily, it would be MOST important for him to describe carefully to the assistant foreman the

    A. previous work experience of each emergency laborer
    B. length of time the assignment is likely to last
    C. nature and extent of the supervisory duties to be assumed
    D. reasons why emergency employees are not as dependable as regular employees

4. Suppose that your district superintendent informs you that several of your men have complained to him about your *unusually strict supervisory methods.*
   In this situation, it would be BEST for you to

    A. ask the superintendent if it is fair for him to let the men go over your head with complaints
    B. ask the superintendent if the men have given him any specific examples of your *strict supervisory methods*
    C. tell the superintendent that you are just doing your job
    D. tell the superintendent that you will try to ease up

5. If an experienced subordinate comes to you for a decision about a problem that he has full authority and the necessary knowledge to solve himself, it would generally be BEST for you to

   A. discuss with him the several alternative solutions to the problem and instruct him to make the decision himself
   B. make the decision but advise him that if this comes up again in the future he must make the decision himself
   C. make the decision without further comment
   D. refuse to discuss the matter and advise him that it is his responsibility to handle this himself

6. At a private conference, your district superintendent discusses with you the failure of your section to keep up with schedules. He remarks that he believes you are saddled with a poor group of men, and he suggests you *push them harder* to get the work done. You sincerely believe that you and your force have done the best possible job with the men and equipment available.
   In this situation, you should

   A. assume full responsibility and blame since you are the boss of the section
   B. explain the circumstances and point out why you feel that you and the men are doing a good job
   C. suggest to the superintendent that he himself speak to the men about the problem
   D. tactfully remind the superintendent that you are closer to the problem than he is

7. The number of subordinates directly reporting to a superior should not be greater than he can supervise competently. This could be an ACCEPTABLE definition of

   A. chain of command   B. span of control
   C. specialized functions   D. unity of command

8. Assume that your district superintendent has issued orders for a change in work procedures that your men disagree with.
   As an officer, it would be BEST for you to tell your men that

   A. nothing can be done about it at this time, even if their complaints are justified
   B. they should complain to the district superintendent, not to you
   C. you did not like the changes yourself and tried to talk the superintendent out of them
   D. you will take up their complaints with the district superintendent

9. Suppose you are going to train your men on a new piece of department equipment.
   In planning your course of instruction, to which one of the following questions should you give FIRST consideration?

   A. Exactly what do I want the men to learn in this course?
   B. How much time should I devote to this instruction?
   C. What assistance can I get in running this training program?
   D. What is the background of the men whom I will instruct?

10. You can pass the buck up but you cannot pass it down. This statement implies MOST directly that an officer

    A. is not responsible for the acts of his subordinates
    B. is responsible for the acts of his subordinates
    C. is responsible for the acts of his superiors
    D. must take the blame for anything he does wrong

11. One of your best workers comes to you to tell you that he wants to quit his job. The FIRST step you should take in handling this matter is to

    A. talk the worker out of quitting
    B. make the worker take time to reconsider the matter
    C. ask the worker why he wants to quit
    D. make the worker's job more interesting

12. An employee you supervise performs a specific job task below the adequate level of efficiency with which he performs the other tasks of his work assignment.
    Of the following, the MOST appropriate FIRST course of action you should take in handling this situation is to

    A. order the worker to *shape up, or else*
    B. remove the specific task from the employee's work assignment
    C. reassign the employee to perform a different work assignment
    D. train the employee to improve his performance on the specific task

13. A foreman thinks that a certain department regulation is unreasonable.
    According to department policy, the BEST one of the following courses of action for him to take if there are repeated infractions of this regulation by his men is for the foreman to

    A. ignore the infractions of this regulation altogether
    B. give lip service reprimands, but never initiate any disciplinary action against the offenders
    C. administer disciplinary action to all guilty men according to the rules and regulations
    D. tell the men that they may ignore this regulation and take the blame himself if anyone is caught

14. Assume that your superior bypasses you in dealing with the employees you supervise.
    Of the following, the MOST accurate statement that can be made concerning this situation is that it is

    A. *good* management practice because it makes those you supervise feel more important
    B. *bad* management practice because it weakens your position to exercise authority
    C. *good* management practice because it gives you more time to do other work
    D. *bad* management practice because it makes the superior's work more unpleasant

15. A foreman observes that an assistant foreman in another foreman's unit uses the strict authoritarian leadership approach in giving orders to his men in that unit.
    Of the following, the BEST course of action for the first foreman to take is for him to

    A. keep from interfering in the matter and offering any advice to the assistant foreman
    B. bring this matter to the attention of the assistant foreman's own superior and let that superior decide if any action is necessary
    C. tell the assistant foreman in private that his leadership approach is wrong and should be changed
    D. discuss the assistant foreman's performance and methods at a meeting with him and several officers to adopt this type of leadership style in your own unit

16. If, after you have been a foreman for several years, you find that your men never complain to you about working conditions or assignments, this is MOST probably a sign that

    A. there is poor communication between you and your men
    B. the men are interested mainly in their rate of pay
    C. the men have nothing to complain about
    D. you are a very good officer

17. In judging the quality of a particular job done by a maintainer, the MOST dependable standard a foreman can use is

    A. the appearance of the finished job
    B. the neatness of the work area while working
    C. how well the completed job holds up in service
    D. how closely instructions were followed in the performance of the job

18. Upon learning that one of your subordinates went to your superior and, by a misrepresentation of facts, obtained his consent to a request you denied, your BEST course of action would be to

    A. demand that the man be brought up on charges
    B. do nothing to avoid prolonging the incident
    C. explain the situation to your superior
    D. request that the man be transferred

19. A foreman of another department complains to you that some of your men did not cooperate fully on a job which was done jointly with his men.
    With respect to this complaint, you should

    A. investigate to substantiate or disprove the charge
    B. ignore the matter because the job is finished
    C. tell the other foreman that your men always cooperate
    D. simply cite instances when his men did not cooperate with you

20. One of your men who has been out sick with a serious illness returns to work and is assigned to his regular duties. After he has been back on the job for about a month, you find that the work of your gang is seriously handicapped by this man's inability to do a full day's work.
It would then be BEST for you to

    A. make arrangements with your superior to have this man examined by the medical department for possible assignment to light duty
    B. give this man about six months' time to get back to normal
    C. tell this man to stay out on sick leave so that you can get an adequate replacement
    D. tell this man that he should stop babying himself and snap out of it

20.___

KEY (CORRECT ANSWERS)

1.	B	11.	C
2.	D	12.	D
3.	C	13.	C
4.	B	14.	B
5.	A	15.	A
6.	B	16.	A
7.	B	17.	C
8.	D	18.	C
9.	A	19.	A
10.	B	20.	A

EXAMINATION SECTION
TEST 1

DIRECTIONS: Each question or incomplete statement is followed by several suggested answers or completions. Select the one that BEST answers the question or completes the statement. *PRINT THE LETTER OF THE CORRECT ANSWER IN THE SPACE AT THE RIGHT.*

1. Foremen should set up work schedules to plan for the most effective use of time, men, and equipment.
   Of the following, the MOST important factor for a foreman to consider in setting up a work schedule is the

   A. seniority of the men assigned to him
   B. salaries of the men needed for the job
   C. availability of men necessary for the job
   D. standard of performance to be attained by his men

2. A newly appointed foreman feels that the use of group participation in the decision-making process will improve the morale and productivity of his men.
   For this foreman to make clear to his men the areas in which group participation will NOT be permitted would generally be considered

   A. *good*, because the men will be unable to take advantage of the foreman
   B. *good*, because certain decisions are beyond the control of both his men and himself
   C. *bad*, because any restraint on the men's freedom of action will dilute the effectiveness of the program
   D. *bad*, because the limitations should be made clear to the group as it becomes involved in a specific area of decision-making

3. Of the following, the LEAST appropriate guide for a foreman to use in assigning his men to various jobs is for him to

   A. assign the work according to his men's ability
   B. allow willing men to take on as many jobs as they wish
   C. combine related jobs and have the same men carry them out
   D. distribute the workload among his men so that no one's load is too light or too heavy.

4. Assume you are foreman of a substation and your relief appears to you to be unfit for duty.
   You should

   A. remain with him until you can determine definitely whether he can perform his duties
   B. allow him to take over since the following tour of duty is not your responsibility
   C. order him off system property and you should remain on duty
   D. make an immediate report to your superior

5. Assume that you have been the foreman in charge of a crew for several weeks when you notice that the men are beginning to show a dislike for you and that this is adversely affecting their morale and efficiency.
Your BEST procedure is to

   A. insist on better discipline
   B. loosen up on the discipline of your crew
   C. take stock of your self to determine whether you are to blame
   D. pay no attention to your crew's attitude as foremen are bound to be disliked no matter what they do

6. A serious accident has occurred involving one of your men on a job to which a foreman had assigned two men.
In questioning both men to fix responsibility, the foreman should be MAINLY interested in obtaining information pertaining to

   A. the ability and experience of each man
   B. how well each man understood his instructions
   C. what each man was doing at the time of the accident
   D. the manner in which the uninjured man usually performs his work

7. In order to prevent accidents, the procedure that is MOST important for a foreman to follow is to

   A. distribute pamphlets, posters, and other training aids
   B. make sure that safe job procedures are observed by his men
   C. hold meetings for discussion of hazards, accidents, and prevention methods
   D. make recommendations to higher management on positive actions for accident prevention

8. Although a foreman need not know every detail of all the jobs that others under him do, he MUST know

   A. what the men under his jurisdiction are capable of handling
   B. which superiors can impart to subordinates the job knowledge that he lacks
   C. how to convince subordinates of his leadership ability despite his lack of overall knowledge
   D. when to transfer the responsibility to subordinates in areas where they are more knowledgeable

9. Assume that a foreman finds his subordinate did a competent job but the foreman is dissatisfied only because he would have done the job differently.
This foreman's BEST course of action would be to

   A. accept this man's method of handling the job
   B. say nothing to this man but watch his work closely in the future
   C. insist that, in the future, this job be done as he would have done it
   D. ask this man questions about other jobs he has done to see whether he always works in this manner

10. A foreman of another department complains to you that some of your men did not cooperate fully on a job done jointly with his men.
    With respect to his complaint, you should

    A. ignore the matter since the job is finished
    B. investigate to substantiate or disprove the charge
    C. tell the other foreman to put his complaint in writing
    D. simply cite instances when you felt his men did not cooperate with your men

11. One of your men goes to your superior and, by a misrepresentation of the facts, obtains his consent to a request you had previously denied.
    As a foreman, you should

    A. request that the man be transferred
    B. ask that the man be brought up on charges
    C. explain the circumstances to your superior
    D. do nothing to avoid prolonging the incident

12. A supervisor assigns a foreman to a special job and asks that certain equipment be used which the foreman believes will not be proper for the intended purpose.
    This foreman should

    A. carry out the instructions without question
    B. discuss this matter with other foremen
    C. discuss his objections with the supervisor
    D. substitute the equipment he believes will be more suitable for the job

13. A maintainer telephones his foreman to report that he cannot find the cause of a particular breaker trouble, describing to the foreman the symptoms and the tests that have been made.
    The foreman's FIRST move should be to

    A. call the system operator
    B. proceed to the location to help
    C. try to diagnose the trouble over the telephone
    D. tell the maintainer to submit a written report immediately

14. As a newly appointed foreman, you find that maintaining all the records turned over to you by your predecessor is taking too much of your time.
    Your BEST action is to

    A. request additional help to relieve you of this problem
    B. discontinue keeping the records you feel are unimportant
    C. stay after regular working hours each week for this purpose
    D. consult your assistant supervisor to see if all the records are necessary

4 (#1)

15. Your supervisor complains to you that he could not find you at your assigned location and your men were idle during the time you were not there.
The MOST important thing for you to do as a result of this incident is to

    A. improve your supervisory practices
    B. disregard such an unreasonable complaint
    C. give an excuse for being away from the job
    D. make certain you are rarely away from your assigned location

16. A foreman starts to give instructions to a maintainer about a certain job and the maintainer tells this foreman that instructions are not necessary since he knows what to do.
This foreman should

    A. question the maintainer as to his intended procedure
    B. let the maintainer proceed without further instructions
    C. keep the maintainer under observation while he is doing the job
    D. insist that the maintainer listen to the full instructions anyway

17. A foreman finds that most of his men have a tendency to bypass him when seeking technical information on details of their work assignments.
The MOST probable reason for this is that his men

    A. are afraid he will reprimand them
    B. want to surprise him with their technical knowledge
    C. do not want him to find out how little they know about their work
    D. either find him not approachable or they have no faith in his technical ability

18. A good foreman should know when to refer a matter to his supervisor and when to handle it himself.
Of the following, the situation which a foreman should APPROPRIATELY refer to his supervisor is a

    A. breakdown of recently purchased equipment
    B. disagreement between two of his maintainers
    C. maintainer consistently returns late from lunch
    D. maintainer who is becoming lax in doing his work

19. A foreman asks a maintainer, who has just completed an assignment, to make certain changes. The maintainer objects because he feels the changes are not necessary. In this case, the foreman should

    A. assign the changes to another maintainer
    B. explain the reasons for the changes to the maintainer
    C. threaten the maintainer with disciplinary action if he doesn't make the changes
    D. tell the maintainer that it is his privilege to take the matter up with the supervisor

20. Of the following, the MOST important advantage of standardizing work procedures is that it

    A. develops all-around skills
    B. makes the work less monotonous
    C. enables the work to be done with less supervision
    D. provides an incentive for better work performances

21. When an unusual situation arises and it would take too long to contact a superior for advice, the MOST practical procedure to follow is to

    A. take no action at all
    B. act according to your best judgment
    C. confer with any other available foremen
    D. confer with all your men on the best action to take

21._____

22. If you, as a foreman, have criticized one of your men for making a mistake, you should

    A. not hold it against him if he does not make this mistake again
    B. tell this man that all his work will be closely checked from now on
    C. remind this man of this mistake from time to time to keep him on his toes
    D. temporarily overlook any other mistakes this man may make since he may feel you are picking on him

22._____

23. If you are assigned by your supervisor to assemble information on a certain power problem, you MUST be especially careful to

    A. be impartial in collecting and presenting the information
    B. secure your information only from those people in supervisory positions
    C. present the information in a way that upholds your supervisor's ideas on the subject
    D. discard any information which might seem inconsistent with previous information relating to this subject

23._____

24. On your first assignment as a newly appointed foreman, one of your most experienced maintainers tells you he wants to discuss an idea which would greatly expedite a certain job.
    Your BEST procedure would be to

    A. discuss and evaluate it with him
    B. adopt his method since he is one of your best men
    C. tell him to see you about it when you have more experience in your title
    D. tell him to submit his idea to your supervisor for approval

24._____

25. Some of your men complain to you about a condition which is common to other departments. They suggest how this condition can be corrected. You feel their suggestion has a great deal of merit although it would involve a drastic change in an established procedure.
    You should

    A. try out this suggestion with your own men first to see how it works
    B. submit this suggestion to your supervisor, with your endorsement, and inform the men of your action
    C. submit this suggestion to the employee suggestion plan with only your name on it since it would carry more weight that way
    D. tell your men that since this is a common problem, if the suggestion were any good, someone would have thought of it before

25._____

KEY (CORRECT ANSWERS)

1.	C	11.	C
2.	B	12.	C
3.	B	13.	C
4.	D	14.	D
5.	C	15.	A
6.	C	16.	A
7.	B	17.	D
8.	A	18.	A
9.	A	19.	B
10.	B	20.	C

21. B
22. A
23. A
24. A
25. B

TEST 2

DIRECTIONS: Each question or incomplete statement is followed by several suggested answers or completions. Select the one that BEST answers the question or completes the statement. *PRINT THE LETTER OF THE CORRECT ANSWER IN THE SPACE AT THE RIGHT.*

1. You are sent by your supervisor to inspect and OK an emergency job on which a cable has been temporarily repaired. After close inspection, you decide the temporary repairs could possibly cause other troubles in a few days if permanent repairs are not made by then.
   In this case, it would be MOST advisable to

   A. OK the job and reinspect it again after a few days
   B. OK the job and inform your supervisor immediately of your finding
   C. refuse to OK the job since permanent repairs may not be made within a few days
   D. refuse to OK the job if you feel permanent repairs could have been made at the time of the emergency

   1.____

2. Just as you are ready to prefer charges against one of your men whose work has been entirely unsatisfactory, you are notified by your supervisor that this man is to be transferred to another foreman.
   In this case, the MOST desirable action for you to take would be to

   A. inform your supervisor of what you are about to do
   B. notify the other foreman of the situation
   C. tell the man what you intended to do and that you are giving him another chance
   D. take no further action since this man's unsatisfactory performance will probably show up in his new position

   2.____

3. As a newly appointed foreman, you find that an experienced maintainer who failed the last promotion examination, which you passed, is bragging to your other men that he is better qualified than you and can show them easier ways of doing certain jobs.
   In this situation, it would be MOST advisable to

   A. praise this maintainer for showing initiative on the job
   B. warn this maintainer to follow your orders in the future and to do the jobs in the prescribed manner
   C. try to get this maintainer a transfer as he will probably continue this practice until the next promotion examination
   D. ignore this maintainer since he is just probably upset about not passing the promotion examination and his attitude will probably soon change

   3.____

4. You find one of your men doing a job which you had not assigned to him. He tells you that he was acting under direct orders of your supervisor.
   In this case, your BEST course of action would be to

   A. tell this man to return to his original assignment and then inform your supervisor of your decision
   B. inform your supervisor that, in the future, you insist on being informed on any change in assignment in advance of such change
   C. tell this man to call the supervisor for an explanation as to why you were bypassed when he assigned this job to him
   D. let this man continue doing the job but contact your supervisor immediately and ask him why the change of assignment was made

   4.____

5. A foreman in charge of a crew of men preparing to work in a danger zone should caution his men to

   A. stay within the limits of the protection provided
   B. consider the dangerous conditions as no deterrent to activities
   C. always work in groups of at least two men
   D. check with him each time they proceed from one step of the job to another

6. In organizing data to be presented in a formal report, the FIRST of the following steps should be

   A. determining the conclusions to be drawn
   B. establishing the time sequence of the data
   C. sorting and arranging like data into groups
   D. evaluating how consistently the data support the recommendations

7. All reports should be prepared with AT LEAST one copy so that

   A. there is one copy for your file
   B. there is a copy for your supervisor
   C. the report can be sent to more than one person
   D. the person getting the report can forward a copy to someone else

8. Before turning in a report of an investigation he has made, a foreman discovers some additional information he did not include in this report.
Whether he rewrites this report to include this additional information should PRIMARILY depend on the

   A. importance of the report itself
   B. number of people who will eventually review this report
   C. established policy covering the subject matter of the report
   D. bearing this new information has on the conclusions of the report

9. Written reports dealing with inspections of work and installations should be

   A. as long and detailed as practicable
   B. phrased with personal interpretations
   C. limited to the important facts of the inspection
   D. technically phrased to create an impression on superiors

10. An ADVANTAGE of written communications as compared to oral communications is the

    A. opportunity provided for ready reference
    B. opportunity provided for immediate feedback
    C. informality of the communications atmosphere
    D. rapidity with which orders can be carried out

11. In giving verbal instructions to a maintainer, a foreman should make them direct and concise MAINLY to

    A. save time
    B. increase the work efficiency of the maintainer
    C. avoid confusing the maintainer
    D. insure the maintainer's attention

12. If a foreman finds that his men have become careless about taking care of minor injuries sustained on the job, he should

    A. eliminate the causes of such injuries
    B. arrange to have the supervisor talk to them
    C. tell them that in the future disciplinary action will be taken
    D. impress on them the danger of infection if injuries are neglected

13. Initially, the BEST way to handle a worker's grievance which you know has very little merit is to

    A. acknowledge the complaint, but do nothing about it
    B. immediately start it through the standard grievance procedure
    C. discuss the grievance with the worker, pointing out its weakness
    D. warn the man that complaints of this sort mark him as a trouble maker

14. A foreman should be prepared for any possible emergency that may arise. In the event of an emergency, it is the responsibility of the foreman to give leadership and direction, and to implement emergency plans in accordance with required safety procedures.
    According to this statement, a foreman should

    A. take no action in an emergency until all safety precautions have been taken
    B. prepare detailed plans in advance for all possible emergencies
    C. take all necessary precautions to prevent emergencies from arising
    D. be prepared to take action in an emergency

15. The MAIN reason for requiring written job reports is to

    A. avoid the necessity of making oral reports on job progress
    B. develop better methods of doing the work
    C. increase the work output
    D. provide a permanent record

16. The BEST way a foreman can help prevent accidents from occurring to his men is to

    A. point out to his men that accidents can be costly in time lost
    B. remind the gang regularly to be safety conscious
    C. post safety notices in spots where the men are likely to see them
    D. watch his men closely and correct them whenever they work in an unsafe manner

17. Assume that you are a foreman and one of your men who works quickly but is very careless has picked into a new gang. His new foreman asks you for your opinion of the man. In replying, you should

    A. point out the man's good qualities only
    B. point out the man's bad characteristics only
    C. point out both the man's good and bad characteristics
    D. avoid committing yourself in order to give the man a chance for a fresh start

18. The BEST way for a foreman to choose a maintainer to do a particularly difficult job is to

    A. give the job to a maintainer who has been goofing off
    B. give the job to a maintainer who has the easiest job in the gang
    C. select the maintainer who is most skilled in the work
    D. ask for a volunteer

19. Employees are required to report defective equipment to their foreman, even when the maintenance of that particular equipment is handled by another department.
    The MAIN purpose of this rule is to

    A. discourage sloppy work
    B. encourage alertness
    C. fix responsibility for carelessness
    D. prevent accidents

20. Advance planning of *fill-in* work for his men is helpful to a foreman MAINLY because he can use it to

    A. keep the men occupied whenever the regular work is delayed
    B. show the men the need for speeding up the regular work
    C. prove to his supervisor that his men do not loaf on the job
    D. justify a request for more men in his gang

21. As a foreman supervising a repair job, you are called away for a few hours.
    Of the following, the BEST action to take before leaving this job site would be for you to

    A. reassign your men to other jobs until you return
    B. assign a man to be in charge during your absence
    C. assign each man enough work to keep him busy until you get back
    D. tell the men you have to leave and you expect the job to be finished when you return

22. You notice a maintainer doing a job in a manner that you believe is unsafe. He tells you that he is doing it the way his previous foreman taught him.
    Of the following, the BEST action for you to take is to

    A. show the maintainer how you want it done
    B. let him continue and see if it turns out all right
    C. reassign the job to someone you know will do it your way
    D. speak to the other foreman to see if the maintainer told you the truth

23. The MOST dependable standard by which a foreman can judge the quality of a particular repair job done by his men is

    A. the number of man-hours it took to do the job
    B. how well the completed job holds up in service
    C. the way his men react to his supervision of the job
    D. how much his instructions were not needed by the men who did the job

24. A supervisor complains to one of his foremen that he could not find him at a particular job site and that the foreman's men did not know where he was.
    Of the following, the MOST important thing for this foreman to do as a result of this incident is to

    A. explain that he was there but nobody called him
    B. improve his supervisory practices
    C. tell his men what happened and ask for their cooperation
    D. make certain he is never away from his job sites in the future

25. On returning from vacation and assuming your duties, you find that your *fill-in* has changed some of your procedures. Of the following, the BEST way to handle this is to

    A. let the matter drop and just reinstate your own procedures
    B. contact this foreman immediately and tell him he had no authority to make any changes
    C. compare this foreman's changes with your procedures and then speak to him about this matter
    D. ask your supervisor to meet with you to find out why changes were made

KEY (CORRECT ANSWERS)

1.	B	11.	C
2.	A	12.	D
3.	B	13.	C
4.	D	14.	D
5.	A	15.	D
6.	C	16.	D
7.	A	17.	C
8.	D	18.	C
9.	C	19.	D
10.	A	20.	A

21.	B
22.	A
23.	B
24.	B
25.	C

EXAMINATION SECTION
TEST 1

DIRECTIONS: Each question or incomplete statement is followed by several suggested answers or completions. Select the one that BEST answers the question or completes the statement. *PRINT THE LETTER OF THE CORRECT ANSWER IN THE SPACE AT THE RIGHT.*

1. Of the following, the one MOST important quality required of a good supervisor is
   A. ambition   B. leadership   C. friendliness   D. popularity

2. It is often said that a supervisor can delegate authority but never responsibility. This means MOST NEARLY that
   A. a supervisor must do his own work if he expects it to be done properly
   B. a supervisor can assign someone else to do his work, but in the last analysis, the supervisor himself must take the blame for any actions followed
   C. authority and responsibility are two separate things that cannot be borne by the same person
   D. it is better for a supervisor never to delegate his authority

3. One of your men who is a habitual complainer asks you to grant him a minor privilege.
   Before granting or denying such a request, you should consider
   A. the merits of the case
   B. that it is good for group morale to grant a request of this nature
   C. the man's seniority
   D. that to deny such a request will lower your standing with the men

4. A supervisory practice on the part of a foreman which is MOST likely to lead to confusion and inefficiency is for him to
   A. give orders verbally directly to the man assigned to the job
   B. issue orders only in writing
   C. follow up his orders after issuing them
   D. relay his orders to the men through co-workers

5. It would be POOR supervision on a foreman's part if he
   A. asked an experienced maintainer for his opinion on the method of doing a special job
   B. make it a policy to avoid criticizing a man in front of his co-workers
   C. consulted his assistant supervisor on unusual problems
   D. allowed a cooling-off period of several days before giving one of his men a deserved reprimand

6. Of the following behavior characteristics of a supervisor, the one that is MOST likely to lower the morale of the men he supervises is
    A. diligence
    B. favoritism
    C. punctuality
    D. thoroughness

7. Of the following, the BEST method of getting an employee who is not working up to his capacity to produce more work is to
    A. have another employee criticize his production
    B. privately criticize his production but encourage him to produce more
    C. criticize his production before his associates
    D. criticize his production and threaten to fire him

8. Of the following, the BEST thing for a supervisor to do when a subordinate has done a very good job is to
    A. tell him to take it easy
    B. praise his work
    C. reduce his workload
    D. say nothing because he may become conceited

9. Your orders to your crew are MOST likely to be followed if you
    A. explain the reasons for these orders
    B. warn that all violators will be punished
    C. promise easy assignments to those who follow these orders best
    D. say that they are for the good of the department

10. In order to be a good supervisor, you should
    A. impress upon your men that you demand perfection in their work at all times
    B. avoid being blamed for your crew's mistakes
    C. impress your superior with your ability
    D. see to it that your men get what they are entitled to

11. In giving instructions to a crew, you should
    A. speak in as loud a tone as possible
    B. speak in a coaxing, persuasive manner
    C. speak quietly, clearly, and courteously
    D. always use the word *please* when giving instructions

12. Of the following factors, the one which is LEAST important in evaluating an employee and his work is his
    A. dependability
    B. quantity of work done
    C. quality of work done
    D. education and training

13. When a District Superintendent first assumes his command, it is LEAST important for him at the beginning to observe
    A. how his equipment is designed and its adaptability
    B. how to reorganize the district for greater efficiency
    C. the capabilities of the men in the district
    D. the methods of operation being employed

14. When making an inspection of one of the buildings under your supervision, the BEST procedure to follow in making a record of the inspection is to
    A. return immediately to the office and write a report from memory
    B. write down all the important facts during or as soon as you complete the inspection
    C. fix in your mind all important facts so that you can repeat them from memory if necessary
    D. fix in your mind all important facts so that you can make out your report at the end of the day

15. Assume that your superior has directed you to make certain changes in your established procedure. After using this modified procedure on several occasions, you find that the original procedure was distinctly superior and you wish to return to it.
    You should
    A. let your superior find this out for himself
    B. simply change back to the original procedure
    C. compile definite data and information to prove your case to your superior
    D. persuade one of the more experienced workers to take this matter up with your superior

16. An inspector visited a large building under construction. He inspected the soil lines at 9 A.M., water lines at 10 A.M., fixtures at 11 A.M., and did his office work in the afternoon. He followed the same pattern daily for weeks.
    This procedure was
    A. *good*, because it was methodical and he did not miss anything
    B. *good*, because it gave equal time to all phases of the plumbing
    C. *bad*, because not enough time was devoted to fixtures
    D. *bad*, because the tradesmen knew when the inspection would occur

17. Assume that one of the foremen in a training course, which you are conducting, proposes a poor solution for a maintenance problem.
    Of the following, the BEST course of action for you to take is to
    A. accept the solution tentatively and correct it during the next class meeting
    B. point out all the defects of this proposed solution and wait until somebody thinks of a better solution
    C. try to get the class to reject this proposed solution and develop a better solution
    D. let the matter pass since somebody will present a better solution as the class work proceeds

18. As a supervisor, you should be seeking ways to improve the efficiency of shop operations by means such as changing established work procedures.
    The following are offered as possible actions that you should consider in changing established work procedures:
    I. Make changes only when your foremen agree to them
    II. Discuss changes with your supervisor before putting them into practice

III. Standardize any operation which is performed on a continuing basis
IV. Make changes quickly and quietly in order to avoid dissent
V. Secure expert guidance before instituting unfamiliar procedures
Of the following suggested answers, the one that describes the actions to be taken to change established work procedures is
   A. I, IV, V   B. II, III, V   C. III, IV, V   D. All of the above

19. A supervisor determined that a foreman, without informing his superior, delegated responsibility for checking time cards to a member of his gang. The supervisor then called the foreman into his office where he reprimanded the foreman.
This action of the supervisor in reprimanding the foreman was
   A. *proper*, because the checking of time cards is the foreman's responsibility and should not be delegated
   B. *proper*, because the foreman did not ask the supervisor for permission to delegate responsibility
   C. *improper*, because the foreman may no longer take the initiative in solving future problems
   D. *improper*, because the supervisor is interfering in a function which is not his responsibility

20. A capable supervisor should check all operations under his control.
Of the following, the LEAST important reason for doing this is to make sure that
   A. operations are being performed as scheduled
   B. he personally observes all operations at all times
   C. all the operations are still needed
   D. his manpower is being utilized efficiently

21. A supervisor makes it a practice to apply fair and firm discipline in all cases of rule infractions, including those of a minor nature.
This practice should PRIMARILY be considered
   A. *bad*, since applying discipline for minor violations is a waste of time
   B. *good*, because not applying discipline for minor infractions can lead to a more serious erosion of discipline
   C. *bad*, because employees do not like to be disciplined for minor violations of the rules
   D. *good*, because violating any rule can cause a dangerous situation to occur

22. A maintainer would PROPERLY consider it poor supervisory practice for a foreman to consult with him on
   A. which of several repair jobs should be scheduled first
   B. how to cope with personal problems at home
   C. whether the neatness of his headquarters can be improved
   D. how to express a suggestion which the maintainer plans to submit formally

23. Assume that you have determined that the work of one of your foremen and the men he supervises is consistently behind schedule. When you discuss this situation with the foreman, he tells you that his men are poor workers and then complains that he must spend all of his time checking on their work.
The following actions are offered for your consideration as possible ways of solving the problem of poor performance of the foreman and his men:
   I. Review the work standards with the foreman and determine whether they are realistic.
   II. Tell the foreman that you will recommend him for the foreman's training course for retraining.
   III. Ask the foreman for the names of the maintainers and then replace them as soon as possible.
   IV. Tell the foreman that you expect him to meet a satisfactory level of performance.
   V. Tell the foreman to insist that his men work overtime to catch up to the schedule.
   VI. Tell the foreman to review the type and amount of training he has given the maintainers.
   VII. Tell the foreman that he will be out of a job if he does not produce on schedule.
   VIII. Avoid all criticism of the foreman and his methods.
   Which of the following suggested answers CORRECTLY lists the proper actions to be taken to solve the problem of poor performance of the foreman and his men?
   A. I, II, IV, VI   B. I, III, V, VII   C. II, III, VI, VIII   D. IV, V, VI, VIII

24. When a conference or a group discussion is tending to turn into a *bull session* without constructive purpose, the BEST action to take is to
   A. reprimand the leader of the bull session
   B. redirect the discussion to the business at hand
   C. dismiss the meeting and reschedule it for another day
   D. allow the bull session to continue

25. Assume that you have been assigned responsibility for a program in which a high production rate is mandatory. From past experience, you know that your foremen do not perform equally well in the various types of jobs given to them. Which of the following methods should you use in selecting foremen for the specific types of work involved in the program?
   A. Leave the method of selecting foremen to your supervisor
   B. Assign each foreman to the work he does best
   C. Allow each foreman to choose his own job
   D. Assign each foreman to a job which will permit him to improve his own abilities

KEY (CORRECT ANSWERS)

1.	B	11.	C
2.	B	12.	D
3.	A	13.	B
4.	D	14.	B
5.	D	15.	C
6.	B	16.	D
7.	B	17.	C
8.	B	18.	B
9.	A	19.	A
10.	D	20.	B

21.	B
22.	A
23.	A
24.	B
25.	B

TEST 2

DIRECTIONS: Each question or incomplete statement is followed by several suggested answers or completions. Select the one that BEST answers the question or completes the statement. *PRINT THE LETTER OF THE CORRECT ANSWER IN THE SPACE AT THE RIGHT.*

1. A foreman who is familiar with modern management principles should know that the one of the following requirements of an administrator which is LEAST important is his ability to
   A. coordinate work
   B. plan, organize, and direct the work under his control
   C. cooperate with others
   D. perform the duties of the employees under his jurisdiction

   1.____

2. When subordinates request his advice in solving problems encountered in their work, a certain chief occasionally answers the request by first asking the subordinate what he thinks should be done.
   This action by the chief is, on the whole,
   A. *desirable*, because it stimulates subordinates to give more thought to the solution of problems encountered
   B. *undesirable*, because it discourages subordinates from asking questions
   C. *desirable*, because it discourages subordinates from asking questions
   D. *undesirable*, because it undermines the confidence of subordinates in the ability of their supervisor

   2.____

3. Of the following factors that may be considered by a unit head in dealing with the tardy subordinate, the one which should be given LEAST consideration is the
   A. frequency with which the employee is tardy
   B. effect of the employee's tardiness upon the work of other employees
   C. willingness of the employee to work overtime when necessary
   D. cause of the employee's tardiness

   3.____

4. The MOST important requirement of a good inspectional report is that it should be
   A. properly addressed   B. lengthy
   C. clear and brief   D. spelled correctly

   4.____

5. Building superintendents frequently inquire about departmental inspectional procedures.
   Of the following, it is BEST to
   A. advise them to write to the department for an official reply
   B. refuse as the inspectional procedure is a restricted matter
   C. briefly explain the procedure to them
   D. avoid the inquiry by changing the subject

   5.____

6. Reprimanding a crew member before other workers is a
   A. *good* practice; the reprimand serves as a warning to the other workers
   B. *bad* practice; people usually resent criticism made in public
   C. *good* practice; the other workers will realize that the supervisor is fair
   D. *bad* practice; the other workers will take sides in the dispute

7. Of the following actions, the one which is LEAST likely to promote good work is for the group leader to
   A. praise workers for doing a good job
   B. call attention to the opportunities for promotion for better workers
   C. threaten to recommend discharge of workers who are below standard
   D. put into practice any good suggestion made by crew members

8. A supervisor notices that a member of his crew has skipped a routine step in his job.
   Of the following, the BEST action for the supervisor to take is to
   A. promptly question the worker about the incident
   B. immediately assign another man to complete the job
   C. bring up the incident the next time the worker asks for a favor
   D. say nothing about the incident but watch the worker carefully in the future

9. Assume you have been told to show a new worker how to operate a piece of equipment.
   Your FIRST step should be to
   A. ask the worker if he has any questions about the equipment
   B. permit the worker to operate the equipment himself while you carefully watch to prevent damage
   C. demonstrate the operation of the equipment for the worker
   D. have the worker read an instruction booklet on the maintenance of the equipment

10. Whenever a new man was assigned to his crew, the supervisor would introduce him to all other crew members, take him on a tour of the plant, tell him about bus schedules and places to eat.
    This practice is
    A. *good*; the new man is made to feel welcome
    B. *bad*; supervisors should not interfere in personal matters
    C. *good*; the new man knows that he can bring his personal problems to the supervisor
    D. *bad*; work time should not be spent on personal matters

11. The MOST important factor in successful leadership is the ability to
    A. obtain instant obedience to all orders
    B. establish friendly personal relations with crew members
    C. avoid disciplining crew members
    D. make crew members want to do what should be done

12. Explaining the reasons for departmental procedure to workers tends to
    A. waste time which should be used for productive purposes
    B. increase their interest in their work
    C. make them more critical of departmental procedures
    D. confuse them

13. If you want a job done well do it yourself.
    For a supervisor to follow this advice would be
    A. *good*; a supervisor is responsible for the work of his crew
    B. *bad*; a supervisor should train his men, not do their work
    C. *good*; a supervisor should be skilled in all jobs assigned to his crew
    D. *bad*; a supervisor loses respect when he works with his hands

14. When a supervisor discovers a mistake in one of the jobs for which his crew is responsible, it is MOST important for him to find out
    A. whether anybody else knows about the mistake
    B. who was to blame for the mistake
    C. how to prevent similar mistakes in the future
    D. whether similar mistakes occurred in the past

15. A supervisor who has to explain a new procedure to his crew should realize that questions from the crew USUALLY show that they
    A. are opposed to the new practice
    B. are completely confused by the explanation
    C. need more training in the new procedure
    D. are interested in the explanation

16. A good way for a supervisor to retain the confidence of his or her employees is to
    A. say as little as possible
    B. check work frequently
    C. make no promises unless they will be fulfilled
    D. never hesitate in giving an answer to any question

17. Good supervision is ESSENTIALLY a matter of
    A. patience in supervising workers   B. care in selecting workers
    C. skill in human relations   D. fairness in disciplining workers

18. It is MOST important for an employee who has been assigned a monotonous task to
    A. perform this task before doing other work
    B. ask another employee to help
    C. perform this task only after all other work has been completed
    D. take measures to prevent mistakes in performing the task

4 (#2)

19. One of your employees has violated a minor agency regulation.
The FIRST thing you should do is
    A. warn the employee that you will have to take disciplinary action if it should happen again
    B. ask the employee to explain his or her actions
    C. inform your supervisor and wait for advice
    D. write a memo describing the incident and place it in the employee's personnel file

19.____

20. One of your employees tells you that he feels you give him much more work than the other employees, and he is having trouble meeting your deadlines.
You should
    A. ask if he has been under a lot of non-work related stress lately
    B. review his recent assignments to determine if he is correct
    C. explain that this is a busy time, but you are dividing the work equally
    D. tell him that he is the most competent employee and that is why he receives more work

20.____

21. A supervisor assigns one of his crew to complete a portion of a job. A short time later, the supervisor notices that the portion has not been completed.
Of the following, the BEST way for the supervisor to handle this is to
    A. ask the crew member why he has not completed the assignment
    B. reprimand the crew member for not obeying orders
    C. assign another crew member to complete the assignment
    D. complete the assignment himself

21.____

22. Supposes that a member of your crew complains that you are *playing favorites* in assigning work.
Of the following, the BEST method of handling the complaint is to
    A. deny it and refuse to discuss the matter with the worker
    B. take the opportunity to tell the worker what is wrong with his work
    C. ask the worker for examples to prove his point and try to clear up any misunderstanding
    D. promise to be more careful in making assignments in the future

22.____

23. A member of your crew comes to you with a complaint. After discussing the matter with him, it is clear that you have convinced him that his complaint was not justified.
At this point, you should
    A. permit him to drop the matter
    B. make him admit his error
    C. pretend to see some justification in his complaint
    D. warn him against making unjustified complaints

23.____

24. Suppose that a supervisor has in his crew an older man who works rather slowly. In other respects, this man is a good worker; he is seldom absent, works carefully, never loafs, and is cooperative.

24.____

The BEST way for the supervisor to handle this worker is to
- A. try to get him to work faster and less carefully
- B. give him the most disagreeable job
- C. request that he be given special training
- D. permit him to work at his own speed

25. Suppose that a member of your crew comes to you with a suggestion he thinks will save time in doing a job. You realize immediately that it won't work.
Under these circumstances, your BEST action would be to
    - A. thank the worker for the suggestion and forget about it
    - B. explain to the worker why you think it won't work
    - C. tell the worker to put the suggestion in writing
    - D. ask the other members of your crew to criticize the suggestion

25.____

KEY (CORRECT ANSWERS)

1.	D		11.	D
2.	A		12.	B
3.	C		13.	B
4.	C		14.	C
5.	C		15.	D
6.	B		16.	C
7.	C		17.	C
8.	A		18.	D
9.	C		19.	B
10.	A		20.	B

21. A
22. C
23. A
24. D
25. B

SUPERVISION, ADMINISTRATION, MANAGEMENT AND ORGANIZATION
EXAMINATION SECTION
TEST 1

DIRECTIONS: Each question or incomplete statement is followed by several suggested answers or completions. Select the one that BEST answers the question or completes the statement. *PRINT THE LETTER OF THE CORRECT ANSWER IN THE SPACE AT THE RIGHT.*

1. The one of the following practices by a supervisor which is MOST likely to lead to confusion and inefficiency is for him to
    A. give orders verbally directly to the man assigned to the job
    B. issue orders only in writing
    C. follow up his orders after issuing them
    D. relay his orders to the men through co-workers

2. If you are given an oral order by a supervisor which you do not understand completely, you should
    A. use your own judgment
    B. discuss the order with your men
    C. ask your supervisor for a further explanation
    D. carry out that part of the order which you do understand and then ask for more information

3. An orientation program for a group of new employees should NOT ordinarily include a
    A. review of the organizational structure of the agency
    B. detailed description of the duties of each new employee
    C. description of the physical layout of the repair shop
    D. statement of the rules pertaining to sick leave, vacation, and holidays

4. The MOST important rule to follow with regard to discipline is that a man should be disciplined
    A. after everyone has had time to "cool off"
    B. as soon as possible after the infraction of rules
    C. only for serious rule violations
    D. before he makes a mistake

5. If the men under your supervision continue to work effectively even when you are out sick for several days, it would MOST probably indicate that
    A. the men are merely trying to show you up
    B. the men are in constant fear of you and are glad you are away
    C. you have trained your men properly and have their full cooperation
    D. you are serving no useful purpose since the men can get along without you

6. When evaluating subordinates, the employee who should be rated HIGHEST by his supervisor is the one who
   A. never lets the supervisor do heavy lifting
   B. asks many questions about the work
   C. makes many suggestions on work procedures
   D. listens to instructions and carries them out

   6._____

7. Of the following, the factor which is generally MOST important to the conduct of successful training is
   A. time   B. preparation   C. equipment   D. space

   7._____

8. One of the MAJOR disadvantages of "on-the-job" training is that it
   A. requires a long training period for instructors
   B. may not be progressive
   C. requires additional equipment
   D. may result in the waste of supplies

   8._____

9. For a supervisor to train workers in several trades which involve various skills, presents many training problems.
   The one of the following which is NOT true in such a training situation is that
   A. less supervision is required
   B. greater planning for training is required
   C. rotation of assignments is necessary
   D. less productivity can be expected

   9._____

10. For a supervisor of repair workers to have each worker specialize in learning a single trade is GENERALLY
    A. *desirable*; each worker will become expert in his assigned trade
    B. *undesirable*; there is less flexibility of assignments possible when each worker has learned only a single trade
    C. *desirable*; the training responsibility of the supervisor is simplified when each worker is required to learn a single trade
    D. *undesirable*; workers lose interest quickly when they know they are expected to learn a single trade

    10._____

11. An IMPORTANT advantage of standardizing work procedures is that it
    A. develops all-around skills
    B. makes the work less monotonous
    C. provides an incentive for good work
    D. enable the work to be done with less supervision

    11._____

12. Generally, the GREATEST difficulty in introducing new work methods is due to the fact that
    A. men become set in their ways
    B. the old way is generally better
    C. only the department will benefit from changes
    D. explaining new methods is time consuming

    12._____

13. Assume that you are required to transmit an order with, which you do not agree, to your subordinates.
    In this case, it would be BEST for you to
    A. ask one of your superiors to transmit the order
    B. refuse to transmit an order with which you do not agree
    C. transmit the order but be sure to explain that you do not agree with it
    D. transmit the order and enforce it to the best of your ability

14. The MAIN reason for written orders is that
    A. proper blame can be placed if the order is not carried out
    B. the order will be carried out faster
    C. the order can be properly analyzed as to its meaning
    D. there will be no doubt as to what the order says

15. You have been informed unofficially by another shop manager that some of the men under your supervision are loafing on the job.
    This situation can be BEST handled by
    A. telling the man to mind his own business
    B. calling the men together and reprimanding them
    C. having the men work under your direct supervision
    D. arranging to make spot checks at more frequent intervals

16. Suggestions on improving methods of doing work, when submitted by a new employee, should be
    A. examined for possible merit because the new man may have a fresh viewpoint
    B. ignored because it would make the old employees resentful
    C. disregarded because he is too unfamiliar with the work
    D. examined only for the purpose of judging the new man

17. One of your employees often slows down the work of his crew by playing practical jokes.
    The BEST way to handle this situation is to
    A. arrange for his assignment to more than his share of unpleasant jobs
    B. warn him that he must stop this practice at once
    C. ignore this situation for he will soon tire of it
    D. ask your supervisor to transfer him

18. One of your men is always complaining about working conditions, equipment, and his fellow workers.
    The BEST action for you to take in this situation is to
    A. have this man work alone if possible
    B. consider each complaint on is merits
    C. tell him bluntly that you will not listen to any of his complaints
    D. give this man the worst jobs until he quits complaining

19. It is generally agreed that men who are interested in their work will do the best work.
    A supervisor can LEAST stimulate this interest by
    A. complimenting men on good work
    B. correcting men on their working procedures
    C. striving to create overtime for his men
    D. recommending merit raises for excellent work

20. If you, as a supervisor, have criticized one of your men for making a mistake, you should
    A. remind the man of his error from time to time to keep him on his toes
    B. overlook any further errors which this man may make, otherwise he may feel he is a victim of discrimination
    C. give the man the opportunity to redeem himself
    D. impress the man with the fact that all his work will be closely checked from then on

21. In his efforts to maintain standards of performance, a shop manager uses a system of close supervision to detect or catch errors.
    An *opposite* method of accomplishing the *same* objective is to employ a program which
    A. instills in each employee a pride of workmanship to do the job correctly the first time
    B. groups each job accordingly to the importance to the overall objectives of the program
    C. makes the control of quality the responsibility of an inspector
    D. emphasizes that there is a "one" best way for an employee to do s specific job

22. Assume that after taking over a repair shop, a shop manager feels that he is taking too much time maintaining records.
    He should
    A. temporarily assign this job to one of his senior repair crew chiefs
    B. get together with his supervisor to determine if all these records are needed
    C. stop keeping those records which he believes are unnecessary
    D. spend a few additional hours each day until his records are current

23. In order to apply performance standards to employees engaged in repair shop activities, a shop manager must FIRST
    A. allow workers to decide for themselves the way to do the job
    B. determine what is acceptable as satisfactory work
    C. separate the more difficult tasks from the simpler tasks
    D. stick to an established work schedule

24. Of the following actions a shop manager can take to determine whether the vehicles used in his shop are being utilized properly, the one which will give him the LEAST meaningful information is
    A. conducting an analysis of vehicle assignments
    B. reviewing the number of miles traveled by each vehicle with and without loads
    C. recording the unloaded weights of each vehicle
    D. comparing the amount of time vehicles are parked at job sites with the time required to travel to and from job sites

25. For a shop manager, the MOST important reason that equipment which is used infrequently should be considered for disposal is that
    A. the time required for its maintenance could be better used elsewhere
    B. such equipment may cause higher management to think that your shop is not busy
    C. the men may resent having to work on such equipment
    D. such equipment usually has a higher breakdown rate in operation

KEY (CORRECT ANSWERS)

1.	D	11.	D
2.	C	12.	A
3.	B	13.	D
4.	B	14.	D
5.	C	15.	D
6.	D	16.	A
7.	B	17.	B
8.	B	18.	B
9.	A	19.	C
10.	B	20.	C

21.	A
22.	B
23.	B
24.	C
25.	A

TEST 2

DIRECTIONS: Each question or incomplete statement is followed by several suggested answers or completions. Select the one that BEST answers the question or completes the statement. *PRINT THE LETTER OF THE CORRECT ANSWER IN THE SPACE AT THE RIGHT.*

1. Assume that one of your subordinates approaches you with a grievance concerning working conditions.
   Of the following, the BEST action for you to take first is to
   A. "soft-soap" him, since most grievances are imaginary
   B. settle the grievance to his satisfaction
   C. try to talk him out of his complaint
   D. listen patiently and sincerely to the complaint

   1.____

2. Of the following, the BEST way for a supervisor to help a subordinate learn a new skill which requires the use of tools is for him to give this subordinate
   A. a list of good books on the subject
   B. lectures on the theoretical aspects of the task
   C. opportunities to watch someone using the tools
   D. opportunities to practice the skill, under close supervision

   2.____

3. A supervisor finds that his own work load is excessive because several of his subordinates are unable to complete their assignments.
   Of the following, the BEST action for him to take to improve this situation is to
   A. discipline these subordinates
   B. work overtime
   C. request additional staff
   D. train these subordinates in more efficient work methods

   3.____

4. The one of the following situations which is MOST likely to be the result of *poor* morale is a(n)
   A. high rate of turnover
   B. decrease in number of requests by subordinates for transfers
   C. increase in the backlog of work
   D. decrease in the rate of absenteeism

   4.____

5. As a supervisor, you find that several of your subordinates are not meeting their deadlines because they are doing work assigned to them by one of your fellow supervisors without your knowledge.
   Of the following, the BEST course of action for you to take in this situation is to
   A. tell the other supervisors to make future assignments through you
   B. assert your authority by publicly telling the other supervisors to stop issuing orders to your workers
   C. go along with this practice; it is an effective way to fully utilize the available manpower
   D. take the matter directly to your immediate supervisor without delay

   5.____

6. If a supervisor of a duplicating section in an agency hears a rumor concerning a change in agency personnel policy through the "grapevine," he should
    A. *repeat* it to his subordinates so they will be informed
    B. *not repeat* it to his subordinates before he determines the facts because, as supervisor, his work may give it unwarranted authority
    C. *repeat* it to his subordinates so that they will like him for confiding in them
    D. *not repeat* it to his subordinates before he determines the facts because a duplicating section is not concerned with matters of policy

6.____

7. When teaching a new employee how to operate a machine, a supervisor should FIRST
    A. let the employee try to operate the machine by himself, since he can learn only by his mistakes
    B. explain the process to him with the use of diagrams before showing him the machine
    C. have him memorize the details of the operation from the manual
    D. explain and demonstrate the various steps in the process, making sure he understands each step

7.____

8. If a subordinate accuses you of always giving him the least desirable assignments, you should IMMEDIATELY
    A. tell him that it is not true and you do not want to hear any more about it
    B. try to get specific details from him, so that you can find out what his impressions are based on
    C. tell him that you distribute assignments in the fairest way possible and he must be mistaken
    D. ask him what current assignment he has that he does not like, and assign it to someone else

8.____

9. Suppose that the production of an operator under your supervision has been unsatisfactory and you have decided to have a talk with him about it.
During the interview, it would be BEST for you to
    A. discuss only the subordinate's weak points so that he can overcome them
    B. discuss only the subordinate's strong points so that he will not become discouraged
    C. compare the subordinate's work with that of his co-workers so that he will know what is expected of him
    D. discuss both his weak and strong points so that he will get a view of his overall performance

9.____

10. Suppose that an operator under your supervision makes a mistake in color on a 2,000-page job and runs it on white paper instead of on blue paper.
Of the following, your BEST course in these circumstances would be to point out the error to the operator and
    A. have the operator rerun the job immediately on blue paper
    B. send the job to the person who ordered it without comment
    C. send the job to the person who ordered it and tell him it could not be done on blue paper
    D. ask the person who ordered the job whether the white paper is acceptable

10.____

11. Assuming that all your subordinates have equal technical competence, the BEST policy for a supervisor to follow when making assignments of undesirable jobs would be to
    A. distribute them as evenly as possible among his subordinates
    B. give them to the subordinate with the poorest attendance record
    C. ask the subordinate with the least seniority to do them
    D. assign them to the subordinate who is least likely to complain

11._____

12. To get the BEST results when training a number of subordinates at the same time, a supervisor should
    A. treat all of them in an identical manner to avoid accusations of favoritism
    B. treat them all fairly, but use different approaches in dealing with people of different personality types
    C. train only one subordinate, and have him train the others, because this will save a lot of the supervisor's time
    D. train first the subordinates who learn quickly so as to make the others think that the operation is easy to learn

12._____

13. Assume that, after a week's vacation, you return to find that one of your subordinates has produced a job which is unsatisfactory.
    Your BEST course of action at that time would be to
    A. talk to your personnel department about implementing disciplinary action
    B. discuss unsatisfactory work in the unit at a meeting with all of your subordinates
    C. discuss the job with the subordinate to determine why he was unable to do it properly
    D. ignore the matter, because it is too late to correct the mistake

13._____

14. Suppose that an operator under your supervision informs you that Mr. Y, a senior administrator in your agency, has been submitting for copying many papers which are obviously personal in nature. The operator wants to know what to do about it, since the duplication of personal papers is against agency rules.
    Your BEST course of action in these circumstances would be to
    A. tell the operator to pretend not to notice the content of the material and continue to copy whatever is given to him
    B. tell the operator that Mr. Y, as a senior administrator, must have gotten special permission to have personal papers duplicated
    C. have the operator refer Mr. Y to you and inform Mr. Y yourself that duplication of personal papers is against agency rules
    D. call Mr. Y's superior and tell him that Mr. Y has been having personal papers duplicated, which is against agency rules

14._____

15. Assume that you are teaching a certain process to an operator under your supervision.
    In order to BEST determine whether he is actually learning what you are teaching, you should ask questions which
    A. can easily be answered by a "yes" or "no"
    B. require or encourage guessing

15._____

C. require a short description of what has been taught
D. are somewhat ambiguous so as to make the learner think about the procedures in question

16. If an employee is chronically late or absent, as his supervisor, it would be BEST for you to
    A. let his work pile up so he can see that no one else will do it for him
    B. discuss the matter with him and stress the importance of finding a solution
    C. threaten to enter a written report on the matter into his personnel file
    D. work out a system with him so he can have a different work schedule than the other employees

17. Assume that you have a subordinate who has just finished a basic training course in the operation of a machine.
    Giving him a large and difficult FIRST assignment would be
    A. *good*, because it would force him to "learn the ropes"
    B. *bad*, because he would probably have difficulty in carrying it out, discouraging him and resulting in a waste of time and supplies
    C. *good*, because how he handles it would give you an excellent basis for judging his competence
    D. *bad*, because he would probably assume that you are discriminating against him

18. After putting a new employee under your supervision through an initial training period, assigning him to work with a more experienced employee for a while would be a
    A. *good* idea, because it would give him the opportunity to observe what he had been taught and to participate in production himself
    B. *bad* idea, because he should not be required to work under the direction of anyone who is not his supervisor
    C. *good* idea, because it would raise the morale of the more experienced employee who could use him to do all the unpleasant chores
    D. *bad* idea, because the best way for him to learn would be to give him full responsibility for assignments right away

19. Assume that a supervisor is responsible for ordering supplies for the duplicating section in his agency.
    Which one of the following actions would be MOST helpful in determining when to place orders so that an adequate supply of materials will be on hand at all times?
    A. Taking an inventory of supplies on hand at least every two months
    B. Asking his subordinates to inform him when they see that supplies are low
    C. Checking the inventory of supplies whenever he has time
    D. Keeping a running inventory of supplies and a record of estimated needs

20. Routine procedures that have worked well in the past should be reviewed periodically by a supervisor MAINLY because
    A. they may have become outdated or in need of revision
    B. employees might dislike the procedures even though they have proven successful in the past
    C. these reviews are the main part of a supervisor's job
    D. this practice serves to give the supervisor an idea of how productive his subordinates are

21. Assume that an employee tells his supervisor about a grievance he has against a co-worker. The supervisor assures the employee that he will immediately take action to eliminate the grievance.
    The supervisor's attitude should be considered
    A. *correct*, because a good supervisor is one who can come to a quick decision
    B. *incorrect*, because the supervisor should have told the employee that he will investigate the grievance and then determine a future course of action
    C. *correct*, because the employee's morale will be higher, resulting in greater productivity
    D. *incorrect*, because the supervisor should remain uninvolved and let the employees settle grievances between themselves

22. If an employee's work output is low and of poor quality due to faulty work habits, the MOST constructive of the following ways for a supervisor to correct this situation generally is to
    A. discipline the employee
    B. transfer the employee to another unit
    C. provide additional training
    D. check the employee's work continuously

23. Assume that it becomes necessary for a supervisor to ask his staff to work overtime.
    Which one of the following techniques is MOST likely to win their willing cooperation to do this?
    A. Explain that this is part of their job specification entitled, "performs related work"
    B. Explain the reason it is necessary for the employees to work overtime
    C. Promise the employees special consideration regarding future leave matters
    D. Explain that if the employees do not work overtime, they will face possible disciplinary action

24. If an employee's work performance has recently fallen below established minimum standards for quality and quantity, the threat of demotion or other disciplinary measures as an attempt to improve this employee's performance would probably be the MOST acceptable and effective course of action
    A. *only* after other more constructive measures have failed
    B. *if* applied uniformly to all employees as soon as performance falls below standard

25. If, as a supervisor, it becomes necessary for you to assign an employee to supervise your unit during your vacation, it would generally be BEST to select the employee who
   A. is the best technician on the staff
   B. can get the work out smoothly, without friction
   C. has the most seniority
   D. is the most popular with the group

25.____

KEY (CORRECT ANSWERS)

1.	D	11.	A
2.	D	12.	B
3.	D	13.	C
4.	A	14.	C
5.	A	15.	C
6.	B	16.	B
7.	D	17.	B
8.	B	18.	A
9.	D	19.	D
10.	D	20.	A

21.	B
22.	C
23.	B
24.	A
25.	B

TEST 3

DIRECTIONS: Each question or incomplete statement is followed by several suggested answers or completions. Select the one that BEST answers the question or completes the statement. *PRINT THE LETTER OF THE CORRECT ANSWER IN THE SPACE AT THE RIGHT.*

1. An employee under your supervision has demonstrated a deep-seated personality problem that has begun to affect his work.
   This situation should be
   A. *ignored*, mainly because such problems usually resolve themselves
   B. *handled*, mainly because the employee should be assisted in seeking professional help
   C. *ignored*, mainly because the employee will consider any advice as interference
   D. *handled*, mainly because the supervisors should be qualified to resolve deep-seated personality problems

2. Of the following, a supervisor will usually be MOST successful in maintaining employee morale while providing effective leadership if he
   A. takes prompt disciplinary action every time it is needed
   B. gives difficult assignments only to those workers who ask for such work
   C. promises his workers anything reasonable they request
   D. relies entirely on his staff for decisions

3. When a supervisor makes an assignment to his subordinates, he should include a clear statement of what results are expected when the assignment is completed.
   Of the following, the BEST reason for following this procedure is that it will
   A. make it unnecessary for the supervisor to check on the progress of the work
   B. stimulate initiative and cooperation on the part of the more responsible workers
   C. give the subordinates a way to judge whether their work is meeting the requirements
   D. give the subordinates the feeling that they have some freedom of action

4. Assume that, on a new employee's first day of work, his supervisor gives him a good orientation by telling him the general regulations and procedures used in the office and introducing him to his department head and fellow employees.
   For the remainder of the day, it would be BEST for the supervisor to
   A. give him steady instruction in all phases of his job, while stressing its most important aspects
   B. have him observe a fellow employee perform the duties of the job
   C. instruct him in that part of the job which he would prefer to learn first
   D. give him a simple task which requires little instruction and allows him to familiarize himself with the surroundings

5. When it becomes necessary to criticize subordinates because several errors in the unit's work have been discovered, the supervisor should USUALLY
   A. focus on the job operation and avoid placing personal blame
   B. make every effort to fix blame and admonish the person responsible
   C. include in the criticism those employees who recognize and rectify their own mistakes
   D. repeat the criticism at regular intervals in order to impress the subordinates with the seriousness of their errors

6. If two employees under your supervision are continually bickering and cannot get along together, the FIRST action that you should take is to
   A. investigate possible ways of separating them
   B. ask your immediate superior for the procedure to follow in this situation
   C. determine the cause of their difficulty
   D. develop a plan and tell both parties to try it

7. In general, it is appropriate to recommend the transfer of an employee for all of the following reasons EXCEPT
   A. rewarding him
   B. providing him with a more challenging job
   C. remedying an error in initial placement
   D. disciplining him

8. Of the following, the MAIN disadvantage of basing a training and development program on a series of lectures is that the lecture technique
   A. does not sufficiently involve trainees in the learning process
   B. is more costly than other methods of training
   C. cannot be used to facilitate the understanding of difficult information
   D. is time consuming and inefficient

9. A supervisor has been assigned to train a new employee who is properly motivated but has made many mistakes.
   In the interview between the supervisor and employee about this problem, the employee should FIRST be
   A. asked if he can think of anything that he can do to improve his work
   B. complimented sincerely on some aspect of his work that is satisfactory
   C. asked to explain why he made the mistake
   D. advised that he may be dismissed if he continues to be careless

10. In training subordinates for more complex work, a supervisor must be aware of the progress that the subordinates are making.
    Determination of the results that have been accomplished by training is a concept commonly known as
    A. reinforcement   B. feedback
    C. cognitive dissonance   D. the halo effect

11. Assume that one of your subordinates loses interest in his work because he feels that your recent evaluation of his performance was unfair.
    The one of the following which is the BEST way to help him is to
    A. establish frequent deadlines for his work
    B. discuss his feelings and attitude with him
    C. discuss with him only the positive aspects of his performance
    D. arrange for his transfer to another unit

12. Informal organizations often develop at work.
    Of the following, the supervisor should realize that these groups will USUALLY
    A. determine work pace through unofficial agreements
    B. restrict vital communication channels
    C. lower morale by providing a chance to spread grievances
    D. provide leaders who will substitute for the supervisor when he is absent

13. Assume that you, the supervisor, have called to your office a subordinate whom, on several recent occasions, you have seen using the office telephone for personal use.
    In this situation, it would be MOST appropriate to begin the interview by
    A. discussing the disciplinary action that you believe to be warranted
    B. asking the subordinate to explain the reason for his personal use of the office telephone
    C. telling the subordinate about other employees who were disciplined for the same offense
    D. informing the subordinate that he is not to use the office telephone under any circumstances until further notice

14. Of the following, the success of any formal training program depends PRIMARILY upon the
    A. efficient and thorough preparation of materials, facilities, and procedures for instruction
    B. training program's practical relevance to the on-the-job situation
    C. scheduling of training sessions so as to minimize interference with normal job responsibilities
    D. creation of a positive initial reception on the part of the trainees

15. All of the following are legitimate purposes for regularly evaluating employee performance EXCEPT
    A. stimulating improvement in performance
    B. developing more accurate standards to be used in future ratings
    C. encouraging a spirit of competition
    D. allowing the employee to set realistic work goals for himself

16. A certain supervisor is very conscientious. He wants to receive personally all reports, correspondence, etc., and to be completely involved in all of the unit's operations. However, he is having difficulty in keeping up with the growing amount of paperwork.

Of the following, the MOST desirable course of action for him to take is to
- A. put in more hours on the job
- B. ask for additional office help
- C. begin to delegate more of his work
- D. inquire of his supervisor if the paperwork is really necessary

17. Assume that you are a supervisor. One of the workers under your supervision expresses his need to speak to you about a client who has been particularly uncooperative in providing information.
The MOST appropriate action for you to take FIRST would be to
- A. agree to see the client for the worker in order to get the information
- B. advise the worker to try several more times to get the information before he asks you for help
- C. tell the worker you will go with him to see the client in order to observe his technique
- D. ask the worker some questions in order to determine the type of help he needs in the situation

18. The supervisor who is MOST likely to achieve a high level of productivity from the professional employees under his supervision is the one who
- A. watches their progress continuously
- B. provides them with just enough information to carry out their assigned tasks
- C. occasionally pitches in and helps them with their work
- D. shares with them responsibility for setting work goals

19. Assume that there has been considerable friction for some time among the workers of a certain unit. The supervisor in charge of this unit becomes aware that the problem is getting serious as shown by increased absenteeism and lateness, loud arguments, etc.
Of the following, the BEST course of action for the supervisor to take FIRST is to
- A. have a staff discussion about objectives and problems
- B. seek out and penalize the apparent trouble-makers
- C. set up and enforce stricter formal rules
- D. discipline the next subordinate who causes friction

20. Assume that an employee under your supervision asks you for some blank paper and pencils to take home to her young grandson who, she says, delights in drawing.
The one of the following actions you SHOULD take is to
- A. give her the material she wants and refrain from any comment
- B. refuse her request and tell her that the use of office supplies for personal reasons is not proper
- C. give her the material but suggest that she buy it next time
- D. tell her to take the material herself since you do not want to know anything about the matter

21. A certain supervisor is given a performance evaluation by his superior. In it he is commended for his method of "delegation," a term that USUALLY refers to the action of
    A. determining the priorities for activities which must be completed
    B. assigning to subordinates some of the duties for which he is responsible
    C. standardizing operations in order to achieve results as close as possible to established goals
    D. dividing the activities necessary to achieve an objective into simple steps

21._____

22. A supervisor is approached by a subordinate who complains that a fellow worker is not assuming his share of the workload and is, therefore, causing more work for others in the office.
    Of the following, the MOST appropriate action for the supervisor to take in response to this complaint is to tell the subordinate
    A. that he will look into the matter
    B. to concentrate on his own job and not to worry about others
    C. to discuss the matter with the other worker
    D. that not everyone is capable of working at the same pace

22._____

23. Aside from the formal relationships established by management, informal and unofficial relationships will be developed among the personnel within an organization.
    Of the following, the MAIN importance of such informal relationships to the operations of the formal organization is that they
    A. reinforce the basic goals of the formal organization
    B. insure the interchangeability of the personnel within the organization
    C. provide an additional channel of communications within the organization
    D. insure predictability and control of the behavior of members of the organization

23._____

24. The most productive worker in a unit frequently takes overly-long coffee breaks and lunch hours while maintaining his above-average rate of productivity.
    Of the following, it would be MOST advisable for the supervisor to
    A. reprimand him, because rules must be enforced equally regardless of the merit of an individual's job performance
    B. ignore the infractions because a superior worker should be granted extra privileges for his efforts
    C. take no action unless others in the unit complain, because a reprimand may hurt the superior worker's feelings and cause him to produce less
    D. tell other members of the unit that a comparable rate of productivity on their part will be rewarded with similar privileges

24._____

25. A supervisor has been asked by his superior to choose an employee to supervise a special project.
Of the following, the MOST significant factor to consider in making this choice is the employee's
   A. length of service
   B. ability to do the job
   C. commitment to the goals of the agency
   D. attitude toward his fellow workers

KEY (CORRECT ANSWERS)

1.	B	11.	B
2.	A	12.	A
3.	C	13.	B
4.	D	14.	B
5.	A	15.	C
6.	C	16.	C
7.	D	17.	D
8.	A	18.	D
9.	B	19.	A
10.	B	20.	B

21.	B
22.	A
23.	C
24.	A
25.	B

TEST 4

DIRECTIONS: Each question or incomplete statement is followed by several suggested answers or completions. Select the one that BEST answers the question or completes the statement. *PRINT THE LETTER OF THE CORRECT ANSWER IN THE SPACE AT THE RIGHT.*

1. Assume that you are a newly appointed supervisor.
   Your MOST important responsibility is to
   A. make certain that all of the employees under your supervision are treated equally
   B. reduce disciplinary situations to a minimum
   C. insure an atmosphere of mutual trust between your workers and yourself
   D. see that the required work is done properly

   1.____

2. In order to make sure that work is completed on time, the supervisor should
   A. pitch in and do as much of the work herself as she can
   B. schedule the work and control its progress
   C. not assign more than one person to any one task
   D. assign the same amount of work to each subordinate

   2.____

3. Assume that you are a supervisor in charge of a number of workers who do the same kind of work and who each produce about the same volume of work in a given period of time.
   When their performance is evaluated, the worker who should be rated as the MOST accurate is the one
   A. whose errors are the easiest to correct
   B. whose errors involve the smallest amount of money
   C. who makes the fewest errors in her work
   D. who makes fewer errors as she becomes more experienced

   3.____

4. As a supervisor, you have been asked by the manager to recommend whether the work of the bookkeeping office requires a permanent increase in bookkeeping office staff.
   Of the following questions, the one whose answer would be MOST likely to assist you in making your recommendation is:
   A. Are temporary employees hired to handle seasonal fluctuations in work loads?
   B. Are some permanent employees working irregular hours because they occasionally work overtime?
   C. Are the present permanent employees keeping the work of the bookkeeping office current?
   D. Are employees complaining that the work is unevenly divided?

   4.____

5. Assume that you are a supervisor. One of your subordinates tells you that he is dissatisfied with his work assignment and that he wishes to discuss the matter with you. The employee is obviously very angry and upset.
Of the following, the course of action that you should take FIRST in this situation is to
   A. promise the employee that you will review all the work assignments in the office to determine whether any changes should be made.
   B. have the employee present his complaint, correcting him whenever he makes what seems to be an erroneous charge against you
   C. postpone discussion of the employee's complaint, explaining to him that the matter can be settled more satisfactory if it is discussed calmly
   D. permit the employee to present his complaint in full, withholding your comments until he has finished making his complaint

5.____

6. Assume that you are a supervisor. You find that you are spending too much time on routine tasks and not enough time on supervision of the work of your subordinates.
It would be ADVISABLE for you to
   A. assign some of the routine tasks to your subordinates
   B. postpone the performance of routine tasks until you have completed your supervisory tasks
   C. delegate the supervisory work to a capable subordinate
   D. eliminate some of the supervisory tasks that you are required to perform

6.____

7. Assume that you are a supervisor. You discover that one of your workers has violated an important rule.
The FIRST course of action for you as the supervisor to take would be to
   A. call a meeting of the entire staff and discuss the matter generally without mentioning any employee by name
   B. arrange to supervise the offending worker's activities more closely
   C. discuss the violation privately with the worker involved
   D. discuss the matter with the worker within hearing of the entire staff so that she will feel too ashamed to commit this violation in the future

7.____

8. As a supervisor, you are to prepare a vacation schedule for the bookkeeping office employees.
The one of the following that is the LEAST important factor for you to consider in setting up this schedule is
   A. seniority   B. vacation preferences of employees
   C. average productivity of the office

8.____

9. In assigning a complicated task to a group of subordinates, a certain supervisor does not indicate the specific steps to be followed in performing the assignment, nor does he designate which subordinate is to be responsible for seeing that the task is done on time.

9.____

This supervisor's method of assigning the task is MOST likely to result in
- A. confusion among subordinates with consequent delays in work
- B. greater individual effort and self-reliance
- C. assumption of authority by capable subordinates
- D. loss of confidence by subordinates in their ability

10. While you are explaining a new procedure to an employee, she asks you a question about the procedure which you cannot answer.
The MOST appropriate action for you to take is to
    - A. admit your inability to answer the question and promise to obtain the information
    - B. point out the likelihood of a situation arising which would require an answer to the question
    - C. ask the worker to give her reason for asking the question before you give any further reply
    - D. tell her to inform you immediately should a situation arise requiring an answer to her question

KEY (CORRECT ANSWERS)

1.	D	6.	A
2.	B	7.	C
3.	C	8.	C
4.	C	9.	A
5.	D	10.	A

PHILOSOPHY, PRINCIPLES, PRACTICES, AND TECHNICS
OF
SUPERVISION, ADMINISTRATION, MANAGEMENT, AND ORGANIZATION

TABLE OF CONTENTS

	Page
MEANING OF SUPERVISION	1
THE OLD AND THE NEW SUPERVISION	1
THE EIGHT (8) BASIC PRINCIPLES OF THE NEW SUPERVISION	1
I. Principle of Responsibility	1
II. Principle of Authority	2
III. Principle of Self-Growth	2
IV. Principle of Individual Worth	2
V. Principle of Creative Leadership	2
VI. Principle of Success and Failure	2
VII. Principle of Science	3
VIII. Principle of Cooperation	3
WHAT IS ADMINISTRATION?	3
I. Practices Commonly Classed as "Supervisory"	3
II. Practices Commonly Classed as "Administrative"	3
III. Practices Commonly Classed as Both "Supervisory" and "Administrative"	4
RESPONSIBILITIES OF THE SUPERVISOR	4
COMPETENCIES OF THE SUPERVISOR	4
THE PROFESSIONAL SUPERVISOR-EMPLOYEE RELATIONSHIP	4
MINI-TEXT IN SUPERVISION, ADMINISTRATION, MANAGEMENT, AND ORGANIZATION	5
I. Brief Highlights	5
A. Levels of Management	6
B. What the Supervisor Must Learn	6
C. A Definition of Supervision	6
D. Elements of the Team Concept	6
E. Principles of Organization	6
F. The Four Important Parts of Every Job	7
G. Principles of Delegation	7
H. Principles of Effective Communications	7
I. Principles of Work Improvement	7
J. Areas of Job Improvement	7
K. Seven Key Points in Making Improvements	8

	L.	Corrective Techniques for Job Improvement	8
	M.	A Planning Checklist	8
	N.	Five Characteristics of Good Directions	9
	O.	Types of Directions	9
	P.	Controls	9
	Q.	Orienting the New Employee	9
	R.	Checklist for Orienting New Employees	9
	S.	Principles of Learning	10
	T.	Causes of Poor Performance	10
	U.	Four Major Steps in On-the-Job Instructions	10
	V.	Employees Want Five Things	10
	W.	Some Don'ts in Regard to Praise	11
	X.	How to Gain Your Workers' Confidence	11
	Y.	Sources of Employee Problems	11
	Z.	The Supervisor's Key to Discipline	11
	AA.	Five Important Processes of Management	12
	BB.	When the Supervisor Fails to Plan	12
	CC.	Fourteen General Principles of Management	12
	DD.	Change	12
II.	Brief Topical Summaries		13
	A.	Who/What is the Supervisor?	13
	B.	The Sociology of Work	13
	C.	Principles and Practices of Supervision	14
	D.	Dynamic Leadership	14
	E.	Processes for Solving Problems	15
	F.	Training for Results	15
	G.	Health, Safety, and Accident Prevention	16
	H.	Equal Employment Opportunity	16
	I.	Improving Communications	16
	J.	Self-Development	17
	K.	Teaching and Training	17
		1. The Teaching Process	17
		a. Preparation	17
		b. Presentation	18
		c. Summary	18
		d. Application	18
		e. Evaluation	18
		2. Teaching Methods	18
		a. Lecture	18
		b. Discussion	18
		c. Demonstration	19
		d. Performance	19
		e. Which Method to Use	19

PHILOSOPHY, PRINCIPLES, PRACTICES, AND TECHNICS
OF
SUPERVISION, ADMINISTRATION, MANAGEMENT, AND ORGANIZATION

MEANING OF SUPERVISION

The extension of the democratic philosophy has been accompanied by an extension in the scope of supervision. Modern leaders and supervisors no longer think of supervision in the narrow sense of being confined chiefly to visiting employees, supplying materials, or rating the staff. They regard supervision as being intimately related to all the concerned agencies of society, they speak of the supervisor's function in terms of "growth," rather than the "improvement" of employees.

This modern concept of supervision may be defined as follows: Supervision is leadership and the development of leadership within groups which are cooperatively engaged in inspection, research, training, guidance, and evaluation.

THE OLD AND THE NEW SUPERVISION

TRADITIONAL
1. Inspection
2. Focused on the employee
3. Visitation
4. Random and haphazard
5. Imposed and authoritarian
6. One person usually

MODERN
1. Study and analysis
2. Focused on aims, materials, methods, supervisors, employees, environment
3. Demonstrations, intervisitation, workshops, directed reading, bulletins, etc.
4. Definitely organized and planned (scientific)
5. Cooperative and democratic
6. Many persons involved (creative)

THE EIGHT (8) BASIC PRINCIPLES OF THE NEW SUPERVISION

I. Principle of Responsibility
   Authority to act and responsibility for acting must be joined.
   A. If you give responsibility, give authority.
   B. Define employee duties clearly.
   C. Protect employees from criticism by others.
   D. Recognize the rights as well as obligations of employees.
   E. Achieve the aims of a democratic society insofar as it is possible within the area of your work.
   F. Establish a situation favorable to training and learning.
   G. Accept ultimate responsibility for everything done in your section, unit, office, division, department.
   H. Good administration and good supervision are inseparable.

II. Principle of Authority
The success of the supervisor is measured by the extent to which the power of authority is not used.
   A. Exercise simplicity and informality in supervision
   B. Use the simplest machinery of supervision
   C. If it is good for the organization as a whole, it is probably justified.
   D. Seldom be arbitrary or authoritative.
   E. Do not base your work on the power of position or of personality.
   F. Permit and encourage the free expression of opinions.

III. Principle of Self-Growth
The success of the supervisor is measured by the extent to which, and the speed with which, he is no longer needed.
   A. Base criticism on principles, not on specifics.
   B. Point out higher activities to employees.
   C. Train for self-thinking by employees to meet new situations.
   D. Stimulate initiative, self-reliance, and individual responsibility
   E. Concentrate on stimulating the growth of employees rather than on removing defects.

IV. Principle of Individual Worth
Respect for the individual is a paramount consideration in supervision.
   A. Be human and sympathetic in dealing with employees.
   B. Don't nag about things to be done.
   C. Recognize the individual differences among employees and seek opportunities to permit best expression of each personality.

V. Principle of Creative Leadership
The best supervision is that which is not apparent to the employee.
   A. Stimulate, don't drive employees to creative action.
   B. Emphasize doing good things.
   C. Encourage employees to do what they do best.
   D. Do not be too greatly concerned with details of subject or method.
   E. Do not be concerned exclusively with immediate problems and activities.
   F. Reveal higher activities and make them both desired and maximally possible.
   G. Determine procedures in the light of each situation but see that these are derived from a sound basic philosophy.
   H. Aid, inspire, and lead so as to liberate the creative spirit latent in all good employees.

VI. Principle of Success and Failure
There are no unsuccessful employees, only unsuccessful supervisors who have failed to give proper leadership.
   A. Adapt suggestions to the capacities, attitudes, and prejudices of employees.
   B. Be gradual, be progressive, be persistent.
   C. Help the employee find the general principle; have the employee apply his own problem to the general principle.
   D. Give adequate appreciation for good work and honest effort.
   E. Anticipate employee difficulties and help to prevent them.
   F. Encourage employees to do the desirable things they will do anyway.
   G. Judge your supervision by the results it secures.

VII. Principle of Science
Successful supervision is scientific, objective, and experimental. It is based on facts, not on prejudices.
   A. Be cumulative in results.
   B. Never divorce your suggestions from the goals of training.
   C. Don't be impatient of results.
   D. Keep all matters on a professional, not a personal, level.
   E. Do not be concerned exclusively with immediate problems and activities.
   F. Use objective means of determining achievement and rating where possible.

VIII. Principle of Cooperation
Supervision is a cooperative enterprise between supervisor and employee.
   A. Begin with conditions as they are.
   B. Ask opinions of all involved when formulating policies.
   C. Organization is as good as its weakest link.
   D. Let employees help to determine policies and department programs.
   E. Be approachable and accessible—physically and mentally.
   F. Develop pleasant social relationships.

WHAT IS ADMINISTRATION

Administration is concerned with providing the environment, the material facilities, and the operational procedures that will promote the maximum growth and development of supervisors and employees. (Organization is an aspect and a concomitant of administration.)

There is no sharp line of demarcation between supervision and administration; these functions are intimately interrelated and, often, overlapping. They are complementary activities.

I. Practices Commonly Classed as "Supervisory"
   A. Conducting employees' conferences
   B. Visiting sections, units, offices, divisions, departments
   C. Arranging for demonstrations
   D. Examining plans
   E. Suggesting professional reading
   F. Interpreting bulletins
   G. Recommending in-service training courses
   H. Encouraging experimentation
   I. Appraising employee morale
   J. Providing for intervisitation

II. Practices Commonly Classified as "Administrative"
   A. Management of the office
   B. Arrangement of schedules for extra duties
   C. Assignment of rooms or areas
   D. Distribution of supplies
   E. Keeping records and reports
   F. Care of audio-visual materials
   G. Keeping inventory records
   H. Checking record cards and books

I. Programming special activities
J. Checking on the attendance and punctuality of employees

III. Practices Commonly Classified as Both "Supervisory" and "Administrative"
   A. Program construction
   B. Testing or evaluating outcomes
   C. Personnel accounting
   D. Ordering instructional materials

RESPONSIBILITIES OF THE SUPERVISOR

A person employed in a supervisory capacity must constantly be able to improve his own efficiency and ability. He represent the employer to the employees and only continuous self-examination can make him a capable supervisor.

Leadership and training are the supervisor's responsibility. An efficient working unit is one in which the employees work with the supervisor. It is his job to bring out the best in his employees. He must always be relaxed, courteous, and calm in his association with his employees. Their feelings are important, and a harsh attitude does not develop the most efficient employees.

COMPETENCES OF THE SUPERVISOR

I. Complete knowledge of the duties and responsibilities of his position.
II. To be able to organize a job, plan ahead, and carry through.
III. To have self-confidence and initiative.
IV. To be able to handle the unexpected situation and make quick decisions.
V. To be able to properly train subordinates in the positions they are best suited for.
VI. To be able to keep good human relations among his subordinates.
VII. To be able to keep good human relations between his subordinates and himself and to earn their respect and trust.

THE PROFESSIONAL SUPERVISOR-EMPLOYEE RELATIONSHIP

There are two kinds of efficiency: one kind is only apparent and is produced in organizations through the exercise of mere discipline; this is but a simulation of the second, or true, efficiency which springs from spontaneous cooperation. If you are a manager, no matter how great or small your responsibility, it is your job, in the final analysis, to create and develop this involuntary cooperation among the people whom you supervise. For, no matter how powerful a combination of money, machines, and materials a company may have, this is a dead and sterile thing without a team of willing, thinking, and articulate people to guide it.

The following 21 points are presented as indicative of the exemplary basic relationship that should exist between supervisor and employee:

1. Each person wants to be liked and respected by his fellow employee and wants to be treated with consideration and respect by his superior.
2. The most competent employee will make an error. However, in a unit where good relations exist between the supervisor and his employees, tenseness and fear do not exist. Thus, errors are not hidden or covered up, and the efficiency of a unit is not impaired.

3. Subordinates resent rules, regulations, or orders that are unreasonable or unexplained.
4. Subordinates are quick to resent unfairness, harshness, injustices, and favoritism.
5. An employee will accept responsibility if he knows that he will be complimented for a job well done, and not too harshly chastised for failure; that his supervisor will check the cause of the failure, and, if it was the supervisor's fault, he will assume the blame therefore. If it was the employee's fault, his supervisor will explain the correct method or means of handling the responsibility.
6. An employee wants to receive credit for a suggestion he has made, that is used. If a suggestion cannot be used, the employee is entitled to an explanation. The supervisor should not say "no" and close the subject.
7. Fear and worry slow up a worker's ability. Poor working environment can impair his physical and mental health. A good supervisor avoids forceful methods, threats, and arguments to get a job done.
8. A forceful supervisor is able to train his employees individually and as a team, and is able to motivate them in the proper channels.
9. A mature supervisor is able to properly evaluate his subordinates and to keep them happy and satisfied.
10. A sensitive supervisor will never patronize his subordinates.
11. A worthy supervisor will respect his employees' confidences.
12. Definite and clear-cut responsibilities should be assigned to each executive.
13. Responsibility should always be coupled with corresponding authority.
14. No change should be made in the scope or responsibilities of a position without a definite understanding to that effect on the part of all persons concerned.
15. No executive or employee, occupying a single position in the organization, should be subject to definite orders from more than one source.
16. Orders should never be given to subordinates over the head of a responsible executive. Rather than do this, the officer in question should be supplanted.
17. Criticisms of subordinates should, whoever possible, be made privately, and in no case should a subordinate be criticized in the presence of executives or employees of equal or lower rank.
18. No dispute or difference between executives or employees as to authority or responsibilities should be considered too trivial for prompt and careful adjudication.
19. Promotions, wage changes, and disciplinary action should always be approved by the executive immediately superior to the one directly responsible.
20. No executive or employee should ever be required, or expected, to be at the same time an assistant to, and critic of, another.
21. Any executive whose work is subject to regular inspection should, wherever practicable, be given the assistance and facilities necessary to enable him to maintain an independent check of the quality of his work.

MINI-TEXT IN SUPERVISION, ADMINISTRATION, MANAGEMENT, AND ORGANIZATION

I. Brief Highlights

Listed concisely and sequentially are major headings and important data in the field for quick recall and review.

A. Levels of Management
Any organization of some size has several levels of management. In terms of a ladder, the levels are:

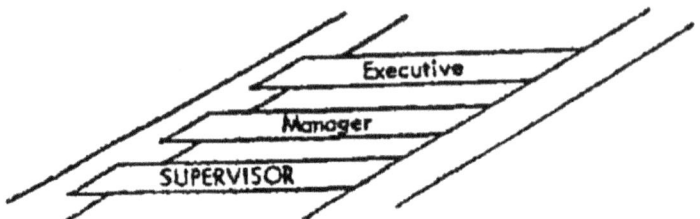

The first level is very important because it is the beginning point of management leadership.

B. What the Supervisor Must Learn
A supervisor must learn to:
1. Deal with people and their differences
2. Get the job done through people
3. Recognize the problems when they exist
4. Overcome obstacles to good performance
5. Evaluate the performance of people
6. Check his own performance in terms of accomplishment

C. A Definition of Supervisor
The term supervisor means any individual having authority, in the interests of the employer, to hire, transfer, suspend, lay-off, recall, promote, discharge, assign, reward, or discipline other employees or responsibility to direct them, or to adjust their grievances, or effectively to recommend such action, if, in connection with the foregoing, exercise of such authority is not of a merely routine or clerical nature but requires the use of independent judgment.

D. Elements of the Team Concept
What is involved in teamwork? The component parts are:
1. Members
2. A leader
3. Goals
4. Plans
5. Cooperation
6. Spirit

E. Principles of Organization
1. A team member must know what his job is.
2. Be sure that the nature and scope of a job are understood.
3. Authority and responsibility should be carefully spelled out.
4. A supervisor should be permitted to make the maximum number of decisions affecting his employees.
5. Employees should report to only one supervisor.
6. A supervisor should direct only as many employees as he can handle effectively.
7. An organization plan should be flexible.

8. Inspection and performance of work should be separate.
9. Organizational problems should receive immediate attention.
10. Assign work in line with ability and experience.

F. The Four Important Parts of Every Job
1. Inherent in every job is the *accountability* for results.
2. A second set of factors in every job is *responsibilities*.
3. Along with duties and responsibilities one must have the *authority* to act within certain limits without obtaining permission to proceed.
4. No job exists in a vacuum. The supervisor is surrounded by key *relationships*.

G. Principles of Delegation
Where work is delegated for the first time, the supervisor should think in terms of these questions:
1. Who is best qualified to do this?
2. Can an employee improve his abilities by doing this?
3. How long should an employee spend on this?
4. Are there any special problems for which he will need guidance?
5. How broad a delegation can I make?

H. Principles of Effective Communications
1. Determine the media.
2. To whom directed?
3. Identification and source authority.
4. Is communication understood?

I. Principles of Work Improvement
1. Most people usually do only the work which is assigned to them.
2. Workers are likely to fit assigned work into the time available to perform it.
3. A good workload usually stimulates output.
4. People usually do their best work when they know that results will be reviewed or inspected.
5. Employees usually feel that someone else is responsible for conditions of work, workplace layout, job methods, type of tools/equipment, and other such factors.
6. Employees are usually defensive about their job security.
7. Employees have natural resistance to change.
8. Employees can support or destroy a supervisor.
9. A supervisor usually earns the respect of his people through his personal example of diligence and efficiency.

J. Areas of Job Improvement
The areas of job improvement are quite numerous, but the most common ones which a supervisor can identify and utilize are:
1. Departmental layout
2. Flow of work
3. Workplace layout
4. Utilization of manpower
5. Work methods
6. Materials handling

7. Utilization
8. Motion economy

K. Seven Key Points in Making Improvements
1. Select the job to be improved
2. Study how it is being done now
3. Question the present method
4. Determine actions to be taken
5. Chart proposed method
6. Get approval and apply
7. Solicit worker participation

L. Corrective Techniques of Job Improvement
Specific Problems
1. Size of workload
2. Inability to meet schedules
3. Strain and fatigue
4. Improper use of men and skills
5. Waste, poor quality, unsafe conditions
6. Bottleneck conditions that hinder output
7. Poor utilization of equipment and machine
8. Efficiency and productivity of labor

General Improvement
1. Departmental layout
2. Flow of work
3. Work plan layout
4. Utilization of manpower
5. Work methods
6. Materials handling
7. Utilization of equipment
8. Motion economy

Corrective Techniques
1. Study with scale model
2. Flow chart study
3. Motion analysis
4. Comparison of units produced to standard allowance
5. Methods analysis
6. Flow chart and equipment study
7. Down time vs. running time
8. Motion analysis

M. A Planning Checklist
1. Objectives
2. Controls
3. Delegations
4. Communications
5. Resources
6. Manpower

7. Equipment
8. Supplies and materials
9. Utilization of time
10. Safety
11. Money
12. Work
13. Timing of improvements

N. Five Characteristics of Good Directions
In order to get results, directions must be:
1. Possible of accomplishment
2. Agreeable with worker interests
3. Related to mission
4. Planned and complete
5. Unmistakably clear

O. Types of Directions
1. Demands or direct orders
2. Requests
3. Suggestion or implication
4. volunteering

P. Controls
A typical listing of the overall areas in which the supervisor should establish controls might be:
1. Manpower
2. Materials
3. Quality of work
4. Quantity of work
5. Time
6. Space
7. Money
8. Methods

Q. Orienting the New Employee
1. Prepare for him
2. Welcome the new employee
3. Orientation for the job
4. Follow-up

R. Checklist for Orienting New Employees   Yes   No
1. Do you appreciate the feelings of new employees
   when they first report for work?   ___   ___
2. Are you aware of the fact that the new employee must
   make a big adjustment to his job?   ___   ___
3. Have you given him good reasons for liking the job and
   the organization?   ___   ___
4. Have you prepared for his first day on the job?   ___   ___
5. Did you welcome him cordially and make him feel needed?   ___   ___

                                                              Yes   No

   6. Did you establish rapport with him so that he feels free
       to talk and discuss matters with you?   ___   ___
   7. Did you explain his job to him and his relationship to you? ___ ___
   8. Does he know that his work will be evaluated periodically
       on a basis that is fair and objective?   ___   ___
   9. Did you introduce him to his fellow workers in such a way
       that they are likely to accept him?   ___   ___
   10. Does he know what employee benefits he will receive?   ___   ___
   11. Does he understand the importance of being on the job
       and what to do if he must leave his duty station?   ___   ___
   12. Has he been impressed with the importance of accident
       prevention and safe practice?   ___   ___
   13. Does he generally know his way around the department? ___   ___
   14. Is he under the guidance of a sponsor who will teach
       the right way of doing things?   ___   ___
   15. Do you plan to follow-up so that he will continue to adjust
       successfully to his job?   ___   ___

S. Principles of Learning
   1. Motivation
   2. Demonstration or explanation
   3. Practice

T. Causes of Poor Performance
   1. Improper training for job
   2. Wrong tools
   3. Inadequate directions
   4. Lack of supervisory follow-up
   5. Poor communications
   6. Lack of standards of performance
   7. Wrong work habits
   8. Low morale
   9. Other

U. Four Major Steps in On-The-Job Instruction
   1. Prepare the worker
   2. Present the operation
   3. Tryout performance
   4. Follow-up

V. Employees Want Five Things
   1. Security
   2. Opportunity
   3. Recognition
   4. Inclusion
   5. Expression

W. Some Don'ts in Regard to Praise
1. Don't praise a person for something he hasn't done.
2. Don't praise a person unless you can be sincere.
3. Don't be sparing in praise just because your superior withholds it from you.
4. Don't let too much time elapse between good performance and recognition of it

X. How to Gain Your Workers' Confidence
Methods of developing confidence include such things as:
1. Knowing the interests, habits, hobbies of employees
2. Admitting your own inadequacies
3. Sharing and telling of confidence in others
4. Supporting people when they are in trouble
5. Delegating matters that can be well handled
6. Being frank and straightforward about problems and working conditions
7. Encouraging others to bring their problems to you
8. Taking action on problems which impede worker progress

Y. Sources of Employee Problems
On-the-job causes might be such things as:
1. A feeling that favoritism is exercised in assignments
2. Assignment of overtime
3. An undue amount of supervision
4. Changing methods or systems
5. Stealing of ideas or trade secrets
6. Lack of interest in job
7. Threat of reduction in force
8. Ignorance or lack of communications
9. Poor equipment
10. Lack of knowing how supervisor feels toward employee
11. Shift assignments

Off-the-job problems might have to do with:
1. Health
2. Finances
3. Housing
4. Family

Z. The Supervisor's Key to Discipline
There are several key points about discipline which the supervisor should keep in mind:
1. Job discipline is one of the disciplines of life and is directed by the supervisor.
2. It is more important to correct an employee fault than to fix blame for it.
3. Employee performance is affected by problems both on the job and off.
4. Sudden or abrupt changes in behavior can be indications of important employee problems.
5. Problems should be dealt with as soon as possible after they are identified.
6. The attitude of the supervisor may have more to do with solving problems than the techniques of problem solving.
7. Correction of employee behavior should be resorted to only after the supervisor is sure that training or counseling will not be helpful.

8. Be sure to document your disciplinary actions.
9. Make sure that you are disciplining on the basis of facts rather than personal feelings.
10. Take each disciplinary step in order, being careful not to make snap judgments, or decisions based on impatience.

AA. Five Important Processes of Management
1. Planning
2. Organizing
3. Scheduling
4. Controlling
5. Motivating

BB. When the Supervisor Fails to Plan
1. Supervisor creates impression of not knowing his job
2. May lead to excessive overtime
3. Job runs itself—supervisor lacks control
4. Deadlines and appointments missed
5. Parts of the work go undone
6. Work interrupted by emergencies
7. Sets a bad example
8. Uneven workload creates peaks and valleys
9. Too much time on minor details at expense of more important tasks

CC. Fourteen General Principles of Management
1. Division of work
2. Authority and responsibility
3. Discipline
4. Unity of command
5. Unity of direction
6. Subordination of individual interest to general interest
7. Remuneration of personnel
8. Centralization
9. Scalar chain
10. Order
11. Equity
12. Stability of tenure of personnel
13. Initiative
14. Esprit de corps

DD. Change

Bringing about change is perhaps attempted more often, and yet less well understood, than anything else the supervisor does. How do people generally react to change? (People tend to resist change that is imposed upon them by other individuals or circumstances.

Change is characteristic of every situation. It is a part of every real endeavor where the efforts of people are concerned.

1. Why do people resist change?
   People may resist change because of:
   a. Fear of the unknown
   b. Implied criticism
   c. Unpleasant experiences in the past
   d. Fear of loss of status
   e. Threat to the ego
   f. Fear of loss of economic stability

2. How can we best overcome the resistance to change?
   In initiating change, take these steps:
   a. Get ready to sell
   b. Identify sources of help
   c. Anticipate objections
   d. Sell benefits
   e. Listen in depth
   f. Follow up

II. Brief Topical Summaries

   A. Who/What is the Supervisor?
      1. The supervisor is often called the "highest level employee and the lowest level manager."
      2. A supervisor is a member of both management and the work group. He acts as a bridge between the two.
      3. Most problems in supervision are in the area of human relations, or people problems.
      4. Employees expect: Respect, opportunity to learn and to advance, and a sense of belonging, and so forth.
      5. Supervisors are responsible for directing people and organizing work. Planning is of paramount importance.
      6. A position description is a set of duties and responsibilities inherent to a given position.
      7. It is important to keep the position description up-to-date and to provide each employee with his own copy.

   B. The Sociology of Work
      1. People are alike in many ways; however, each individual is unique.
      2. The supervisor is challenged in getting to know employee differences. Acquiring skills in evaluating individuals is an asset.
      3. Maintaining meaningful working relationships in the organization is of great importance.
      4. The supervisor has an obligation to help individuals to develop to their fullest potential.
      5. Job rotation on a planned basis helps to build versatility and to maintain interest and enthusiasm in work groups.
      6. Cross training (job rotation) provides backup skills.

7. The supervisor can help reduce tension by maintaining a sense of humor, providing guidance to employees, and by making reasonable and timely decisions. Employees respond favorably to working under reasonably predictable circumstances.
8. Change is characteristic of all managerial behavior. The supervisor must adjust to changes in procedures, new methods, technological changes, and to a number of new and sometimes challenging situations.
9. To overcome the natural tendency for people to resist change, the supervisor should become more skillful in initiating change.

C. Principles and Practices of Supervision
1. Employees should be required to answer to only one superior.
2. A supervisor can effectively direct only a limited number of employees, depending upon the complexity, variety, and proximity of the jobs involved.
3. The organizational chart presents the organization in graphic form. It reflects lines of authority and responsibility as well as interrelationships of units within the organization.
4. Distribution of work can be improved through an analysis using the "Work Distribution Chart."
5. The "Work Distribution Chart" reflects the division of work within a unit in understandable form.
6. When related tasks are given to an employee, he has a better chance of increasing his skills through training.
7. The individual who is given the responsibility for tasks must also be given the appropriate authority to insure adequate results.
8. The supervisor should delegate repetitive, routine work. Preparation of recurring reports, maintaining leave and attendance records are some examples.
9. Good discipline is essential to good task performance. Discipline is reflected in the actions of employees on the job in the absence of supervision.
10. Disciplinary action may have to be taken when the positive aspects of discipline have failed. Reprimand, warning, and suspension are examples of disciplinary action.
11. If a situation calls for a reprimand, be sure it is deserved and remember it is to be done in private.

D. Dynamic Leadership
1. A style is a personal method or manner of exerting influence.
2. Authoritarian leaders often see themselves as the source of power and authority.
3. The democratic leader often perceives the group as the source of authority and power.
4. Supervisors tend to do better when using the pattern of leadership that is most natural for them.
5. Social scientists suggest that the effective supervisor use the leadership style that best fits the problem or circumstances involved.
6. All four styles—telling, selling, consulting, joining—have their place. Using one does not preclude using the other at another time.

7. The theory X point of view assumes that the average person dislikes work, will avoid it whenever possible, and must be coerced to achieve organizational objectives.
8. The theory Y point of view assumes that the average person considers work to be a natural as play, and, when the individual is committed, he requires little supervision or direction to accomplish desired objectives.
9. The leader's basic assumptions concerning human behavior and human nature affect his actions, decisions, and other managerial practices.
10. Dissatisfaction among employees is often present, but difficult to isolate. The supervisor should seek to weaken dissatisfaction by keeping promises, being sincere and considerate, keeping employees informed, and so forth.
11. Constructive suggestions should be encouraged during the natural progress of the work.

E. Processes for Solving Problems
1. People find their daily tasks more meaningful and satisfying when they can improve them.
2. The causes of problems, or the key factors, are often hidden in the background. Ability to solve problems often involves the ability to isolate them from their backgrounds. There is some substance to the cliché that some persons "can't see the forest for the trees."
3. New procedures are often developed from old ones. Problems should be broken down into manageable parts. New ideas can be adapted from old one.
4. People think differently in problem-solving situations. Using a logical, patterned approach is often useful. One approach found to be useful includes these steps:
   a. Define the problem
   b. Establish objectives
   c. Get the facts
   d. Weigh and decide
   e. Take action
   f. Evaluate action

F. Training for Results
1. Participants respond best when they feel training is important to them.
2. The supervisor has responsibility for the training and development of those who report to him.
3. When training is delegated to others, great care must be exercised to insure the trainer has knowledge, aptitude, and interest for his work as a trainer.
4. Training (learning) of some type goes on continually. The most successful supervisor makes certain the learning contributes in a productive manner to operational goals.
5. New employees are particularly susceptible to training. Older employees facing new job situations require specific training, as well as having need for development and growth opportunities.
6. Training needs require continuous monitoring.
7. The training officer of an agency is a professional with a responsibility to assist supervisors in solving training problems.

8. Many of the self-development steps important to the supervisor's own growth are equally important to the development of peers and subordinates. Knowledge of these is important when the supervisor consults with others on development and growth opportunities.

G. Health, Safety, and Accident Prevention
1. Management-minded supervisors take appropriate measures to assist employees in maintaining health and in assuring safe practices in the work environment.
2. Effective safety training and practices help to avoid injury and accidents.
3. Safety should be a management goal. All infractions of safety which are observed should be corrected without exception.
4. Employees' safety attitude, training and instruction, provision of safe tools and equipment, supervision, and leadership are considered highly important factors which contribute to safety and which can be influenced directly by supervisors.
5. When accidents do occur, they should be investigated promptly for very important reasons, including the fact that information which is gained can be used to prevent accidents in the future.

H. Equal Employment Opportunity
1. The supervisor should endeavor to treat all employees fairly, without regard to religion, race, sex, or national origin.
2. Groups tend to reflect the attitude of the leader. Prejudice can be detected even in very subtle form. Supervisors must strive to create a feeling of mutual respect and confidence in every employee.
3. Complete utilization of all human resources is a national goal. Equitable consideration should be accorded women in the work force, minority-group members, the physically and mentally handicapped, and the older employee. The important question is: "Who can do the job?"
4. Training opportunities, recognition for performance, overtime assignments, promotional opportunities, and all other personnel actions are to be handled on an equitable basis.

I. Improving Communications
1. Communications is achieving understanding between the sender and the receiver of a message. It also means sharing information—the creation of understanding.
2. Communication is basic to all human activity. Words are means of conveying meanings; however, real meanings are in people.
3. There are very practical differences in the effectiveness of one-way, impersonal, and two-way communications. Words spoken face-to-face are better understood. Telephone conversations are effective, but lack the rapport of person-to-person exchanges. The whole person communicates.
4. Cooperation and communication in an organization go hand in hand. When there is a mutual respect between people, spelling out rules and procedures for communicating is unnecessary.
5. There are several barriers to effective communications. These include failure to listen with respect and understanding, lack of skill in feedback, and misinterpreting the meanings of words used by the speaker. It is also common

practice to listen to what we want to hear, and tune out things we do not want to hear.
6. Communication is management's chief problem. The supervisor should accept the challenge to communicate more effectively and to improve interagency and intra-agency communications.
7. The supervisor may often plan for and conduct meetings. The planning phase is critical and may determine the success or the failure of a meeting.
8. Speaking before groups usually requires extra effort. Stage fright may never disappear completely, but it can be controlled.

J. Self-Development
1. Every employee is responsible for his own self-development.
2. Toastmaster and toastmistress clubs offer opportunities to improve skills in oral communications.
3. Planning for one's own self-development is of vital importance. Supervisors know their own strengths and limitations better than anyone else.
4. Many opportunities are open to aid the supervisor in his developmental efforts, including job assignments; training opportunities, both governmental and non-governmental—to include universities and professional conferences and seminars.
5. Programmed instruction offers a means of studying at one's own rate.
6. Where difficulties may arise from a supervisor's being away from his work for training, he may participate in televised home study or correspondence courses to meet his self-development needs.

K. Teaching and Training
1. The Teaching Process
Teaching is encouraging and guiding the learning activities of students toward established goals. In most cases this process consists of five steps: preparation, presentation, summarization, evaluation, and application.

   a. Preparation
   Preparation is two-fold in nature; that of the supervisor and the employee. Preparation by the supervisor is absolutely essential to success. He must know what, when, where, how, and whom he will teach. Some of the factors that should be considered are:
   1) The objectives
   2) The materials needed
   3) The methods to be used
   4) Employee participation
   5) Employee interest
   6) Training aids
   7) Evaluation
   8) Summarization

   Employee preparation consists in preparing the employee to receive the material. Probably the most important single factor in the preparation of the employee is arousing and maintaining his interest. He must know the objectives of the training, why he is there, how the material can be used, and its importance to him.

b. Presentation
In presentation, have a carefully designed plan and follow it. The plan should be accurate and complete, yet flexible enough to meet situations as they arise. The method of presentation will be determined by the particular situation and objectives.

c. Summary
A summary should be made at the end of every training unit and program. In addition, there may be internal summaries depending on the nature of the material being taught. The important thing is that the trainee must always be able to understand how each part of the new material relates to the whole.

d. Application
The supervisor must arrange work so the employee will be given a chance to apply new knowledge or skills while the material is still clear in his mind and interest is high. The trainee does not really know whether he has learned the material until he has been given a chance to apply it. If the material is not applied, it loses most of its value.

e. Evaluation
The purpose of all training is to promote learning. To determine whether the training has been a success or failure, the supervisor must evaluate this learning.
In the broadest sense, evaluation includes all the devices, methods, skills, and techniques used by the supervisor to keep himself and the employees informed as to their progress toward the objectives they are pursuing. The extent to which the employee has mastered the knowledge, skills, and abilities, or changed his attitudes, as determined by the program objectives, is the extent to which instruction has succeeded or failed.
Evaluation should not be confined to the end of the lesson, day, or program but should be used continuously. We shall note later the way this relates to the rest of the teaching process.

2. Teaching Methods
A teaching method is a pattern of identifiable student and instructor activity used in presenting training material.
All supervisors are faced with the problem of deciding which method should be used at a given time.

a. Lecture
The lecture is direct oral presentation of material by the supervisor. The present trend is to place less emphasis on the trainer's activity and more on that of the trainee.

b. Discussion
Teaching by discussion or conference involves using questions and other techniques to arouse interest and focus attention upon certain areas, and by doing so creating a learning situation. This can be one of the most

valuable methods because it gives the employees an opportunity to express their ideas and pool their knowledge.

    c. Demonstration
The demonstration is used to teach how something works or how to do something. It can be used to show a principle or what the results of a series of actions will be. A well-staged demonstration is particularly effective because it shows proper methods of performance in a realistic manner.

    d. Performance
Performance is one of the most fundamental of all learning techniques or teaching methods. The trainee may be able to tell how a specific operation should be performed but he cannot be sure he knows how to perform the operation until he has done so.
As with all methods, there are certain advantages and disadvantages to each method.

    e. Which Method to Use
Moreover, there are other methods and techniques of teaching. It is difficult to use any method without other methods entering into it. In any learning situation, a combination of methods is usually more effective than any one method alone.

Finally, evaluation must be integrated into the other aspects of the teaching-learning process.

It must be used in the motivation of the trainees; it must be used to assist in developing understanding during the training; and it must be related to employee application of the results of training.

This is distinctly the role of the supervisor.

www.ingramcontent.com/pod-product-compliance
Lightning Source LLC
Chambersburg PA
CBHW082045300426
44117CB00015B/2618